T0058389

TROUT TIPS

TROUT

TROUT TIPS

MORE THAN 250 FLY-FISHING TIPS
FROM THE MEMBERS OF TROUT UNLIMITED

Edited by Kirk Deeter

Skyhorse Publishing

Skyhorse Publishing books may be purchased in bulk at special discounts for sales promotion, corporate gifts, fund-raising, or educational purposes. Special editions can also be created to specifications. For details, contact the Special Sales Department, Skyhorse Publishing, 307 West 36th Street, 11th Floor, New York, NY 10018 or info@skyhorsepublishing.com.

Skyhorse® and Skyhorse Publishing® are registered trademarks of Skyhorse Publishing, Inc.®, a Delaware corporation.

Visit our website at www.skyhorsepublishing.com.

10 9 8 7 6 5 4

Library of Congress Cataloging-in-Publication Data is available on file.

Cover design by Tom Lau
Cover photo credit: Tim Romano, courtesy of Scientific Anglers
Interior illustrations courtesy of Rod Walinchus

Print ISBN: 978-1-5107-1370-3
Ebook ISBN: 978-1-5107-1371-0

Printed in China

*THIS BOOK IS DEDICATED TO THE MANY CURRENT
AND PAST MEMBERS OF TROUT UNLIMITED WHO HAVE
DONE, AND CONTINUE TO DO, THE EXTRAORDINARY
WORK THAT MAKES TROUT FISHING POSSIBLE IN THE
FIRST PLACE.THANK YOU.*

"Take care of the fish, and the fishing will take care of itself."
—Art Neumann, co-founder of Trout Unlimited

Contents

Acknowledgments

This book is a true group effort, and the culmination of many river miles, waded and fished by many friends, colleagues, and kindred spirits. Thanks to all the TU staffers and volunteers around the country who pulled together to make this book possible. Special thanks to Chris Wood, president and CEO of TU, for having faith in the project to begin with, and to the Trout Media staff, especially Samantha Carmichael, Erin Block, and Jim Gray, for their support. I also want to thank my friends at *Field & Stream* magazine for their flexibility and the opportunity to write for the leading outdoors media brand in the world. Thank you to my business partner and good friend Tim Romano, Mr. Reliable. Thanks to my editor and friend Jay Cassell, who has been my editor and friend for many years before we tackled this project (and we're still pals!). Last, but not least, thanks to my very supportive family, especially my wife, Sarah, and son, Paul, with whom I enjoy chasing trout in wild places most of all.

Foreword

My high school basketball coach from Jersey City once told me, "you may think you're a pretty good ball player, but I can go to any street corner in this city, and find someone who can beat you in one on one. It is the fact that you are part of a team that makes us all better." The same could be said for fly-fishing. Most of us know how to get the line on the water. We know, generally, where to find fish. We are all fairly proficient at putting the bugs the TU business fly-shop sold us where they need to go. But much like a basketball team, we become better anglers when we take the time to learn from others who share our passion.

Trout Unlimited has more than 220 staff and 400 chapters spread all across the country who work in common cause toward a specific goal: to make your fishing better. That is what makes it so heartwarming to see these tips from all over the country—men, women, kids, novice anglers, old-hands—that's the Trout Unlimited family at work, and everyone plays a part. The book is a reflection of Trout Unlimited's belief that "many hands" make heavy lifting easy.

But the bottom line is that you can cast 100 feet, tie the deadliest pattern in the world, and make it swim prettier than Michael Phelps, but none of that matters if there are not fish in the water. So, if you are already a supporter of Trout Unlimited, thank you. If not, and you love to fish, and want to surround yourself with others who will make you a better angler and help you to give back to this resource we all love, join Trout Unlimited today.

—Chris Wood,
CEO of Trout Unlimited

Introduction

I have always felt that fly fishing for trout is ultimately less about flies and trout, and more about the people you meet, and the places you experience along the way.

That's not to say that I don't appreciate the unique tranquility that can only be found on a river with a fly line whispering a four-count rhythm overhead, and cool water pressing around my legs. And I like the tug a trout makes, particularly after they've risen for a dry fly. A lot.

But it seems to me that, while I might snap some fish photos along the way, at the end of the day or at the end of the trip, I don't remember the fish as much as I remember the place and the person (or people) I was fishing with. Even fishing in total solitude, I remember the person I was *thinking* about—the one who taught me *this* trick or inspired me to find *that* place. One of the most beautiful aspects of fly fishing for trout is that you are never truly alone. You are always part of something larger than yourself. Nature . . . tradition . . . community.

Having had the good fortune to fish many rivers throughout North America and beyond, I have grown particularly fascinated with lifting tips from one watershed and trying to apply them to another. Will this killer fly pattern from the Madison work on the Delaware, as well? Will I find a trout holding in that subtle seam on the Pere Marquette, just like I did on the Deschutes? I wonder if I can skate this bug on Silver Creek like I did on the Upper Colorado . . .

As with all things fly fishing, the answer to these questions is usually a "definite maybe."

Several years ago, I wrote a book with my outdoor writing mentor, the late, great Charlie Meyers, former outdoors columnist for the *Denver Post*. It's called *The Little Red Book of Fly Fishing*. And it has done very well, because it was all about "definite maybes." Charlie had rolled and fished enough rivers in his day to know that nothing is an absolute. (He thought, for example, that anyone who professed to be an *all-knowing* guru on any aspect of fly fishing was, in truth, an absolute nut. And I agreed with him.) The smartest anglers realize that the more they fish, the more they can still learn.

Sure, there are some fundamentals to share (like scales and chords for the musician), but good fishing is always about improvisation, and playing to the beat you hear in your head. As reporters, Charlie and I merely shared tips and tricks we picked up in our collective travels. Usually, we agreed. Sometimes we contradicted each other . . . on purpose. It was important to let the reader sort it out for himself or herself.

After all, fly fishing for trout is problem solving. "How do I get this fly into the mouth of that fish swimming 40 feet away from me?" If there were a step-by-step instruction manual that explained how to solve that problem, every time, nobody would want to read it, and nobody would want to fish.

Charlie is gone now, and I think about him, at least for a little bit, pretty much every time I go fishing. I've seen new waters in great places, and more important, I have met many other wonderful people who continue to shape the way I fish and think about fly fishing for trout.

Central to all of that has been my "homecoming" of sorts, assuming the role of editor of *Trout* magazine and working for Trout Unlimited, the organization that does so much to make trout fishing (of all types, not just fly fishing) possible in the first place. One thing that *is* an absolute, at least in my mind, is that every angler should have a conscience, and "conservation" in the trout-angling context is a far deeper ideal than letting the little ones go to fight another day.

It is therefore worth noting that *all* the author royalties are going directly back into Trout Unlimited, with the hope of making fishing better for everyone. That's as much soapbox speak as you're going to find in the pages that follow. Please take that for what it's worth.

I have thousands of new partners now in the TU community. And you will read many of their voices here. The goal with this book is to help you become a better angler, period. And you'll see tips and tricks from different anglers, from all sorts of waters in different places throughout North America and beyond, that will help you get there.

To be clear, this is not a "guidebook" or a fly-fishing "manual." There are plenty of those already. It's not a book on fish (specifically trout). We will get to that later. It isn't a fly-tying book, though there are a few tying thoughts covered here. It's a book of tips. A bag of tricks. Some for the novice, others for experts. By anglers, for anglers. And that's about it.

To keep things organized, we break fly fishing for trout into four simple categories: casting a fly rod . . . choosing a fly to catch a trout . . . reading water (so you know where to put that fly in the first place) . . . and "presentation," which is the art of showing that fly to trout in a way that will make the fish want to eat it. Simple stuff.

We will dabble some on rigs and gear. There's a bit on fighting fish and how catch-and-release anglers can best handle them. Homespun tricks. New ideas. Old standards. All fair game. We focus on fly fishing, because that's what most of us know best. But we fully recognize that there are many ways to catch trout, all worthy and wonderful. (Does anyone else smell a possible sequel?)

Sometimes, you'll read similar tips from different people. That redundancy is intentional. If you read that someone in Alaska and another angler from Georgia have a similar approach to reading water, for example, you should consider that fairly powerful food for thought.

We're going to disagree with each other, too. Some people, for example, say you can't catch fish if your fly isn't on the water. Others contend that one well-reasoned, sharply executed shot is worth one thousand "Hail Mary" casts.

I'm not the referee; I'm the editor. You are the referee. You can make notes in the book and be as much a part of this writing team as anyone else, if you want to be. And feel free, by the way, to hand this book off, with your notes included, to another angler who you think might benefit from the insight.

As with everything TU does, this is a work in process. The more you take part in the process, appreciating the fishing—as well as the people and places along the way—the better, more fulfilled angler you will become.

I promise.

Thank you for playing your part.

—Kirk Deeter
Pine, Colorado
2016

CHAPTER 1

10 Things You Should Know about Casting a Fly Rod

Casting is what gets the most attention in fly fishing, for better or worse. There have probably been more books written on casting than on any other aspect of fly fishing, because it is the most "visible" element of the sport. If you ask most newbie fly anglers what intimidates them most, it's the cast. If you ask lifelong "experts" what frustrates them the most . . . it's the cast.

The cast is the starting point, akin to the drive you hit from the first tee on a golf course. A great cast is a beautiful thing. It feels good when you shoot that line directly where you want it. When you make a great cast, and are rewarded with a good trout, that's the top of the game.

But the cast is not the only price of admission. Aspire to cast well; a great cast will never, ever hurt your chances (and poor casts will certainly wreck opportunities). But there's casting, and then there's fishing. And some of the best trout anglers are mediocre casters on their best day. And that's just fine.

The point being, no one should be preoccupied with the cast to the exclusion of the many other facets of fly fishing. And they shouldn't ever be ashamed of a cast that might not have textbook looks but still drops the fly on the money.

Here are some basic principles that apply to all anglers, from novice to expert, which will help you get more out of your casts:

1. You're Throwing a Weight, and You Should Feel That

Granted, that "weight" looks like a 90-foot-long piece of spaghetti. But unlike conventional fishing, where the weight is concentrated in the lure (or the bait) you cast and the line itself is virtually weightless, in fly fishing, the flies weigh very little, and the line itself contains the mass. That's key, because you need to be in the mind-set that the long fly rod you are using (and they make the average fly rod 9 feet long for a reason) is a launcher, specifically designed to help you throw that weighted line.

But you need to be thinking about your fly line as much or more than you are the fly rod. One of the best practice tips is try and "cast" the fly line using only your hand. Done right, you can feel that weight extend behind you, and that sudden *tunk* will tell you when to transfer the energy and move the cast forward. Some expert casters can actually throw more than half a fly line without a rod at all. When you add the fly rod to the mix, casting naturally gets a whole lot easier. But it starts with feeling that weight transfer in your bare hand. A great rod will help you do that, but there is no substitute for practice.

2. Casting is about Accelerating and Stopping

A fly rod—and a fly cast—only works if you get in your mind the importance of accelerating through the stroke, and then stopping the rod. Most of us are taught to cast by imagining swinging the rod back and forth, as if we were standing in an imaginary clock face and we want our backcast to stop at 10 o'clock (if we are facing toward 3 o'clock) and end at 2 o'clock. That's true. But if we're sloughing our way between 10 and 2, it's not going to happen. Accelerate from 10 to 2 (and stop that rod tip, crisply, almost exactly at the appointed hour).

There are hundreds of metaphors to explain this feel. Imagine banging a rubber mallet between two solid boards, about 2 feet apart. Bang the board over your shoulder, then bang the one in front of you. Accelerate and stop.

Imagine lifting a glass of water off a table and throwing that water over your shoulder. Do it all at once, and you only get wet. If you don't stop, the water pours over your shoulder. Accelerate and stop, and you can fling that water quite a ways.

My favorite remains the "tomato on a stick" description. Imagine a ripe tomato stuck to the end of your fly rod. If you want to throw it, you need to accelerate (and feel the flex in the rod as it loads), and then stop the rod so the tomato flings off the end. Do it too abruptly, and you're covered in gazpacho. Do it too meekly, and the tomato never takes off. Accelerate and stop, and you're an expert tomato chucker . . . and eventually a great fly caster.

Accelerate and stop the rod, both on the backcast and the forward cast.

3. It's Never about Raw Power

One of the greatest challenges fly-casting instructors face as they teach men to cast is trying to undo the effects of testosterone. That's why most women are better natural-born fly casters than most men. Having just said what we did about throwing weight, accelerating, and stopping, it's important that you not confuse any of that with "punching" or "pushing" or "pounding" a cast. Like a great, grooved golf swing, a great fly cast is all about timing and tempo, and it has very little to do with sheer muscle.

The best drill to demonstrate that is the "take flight" exercise. Strip out about 30 feet of line (out the end of your rod) and put it in a pile in front of you. Now gently start moving the rod back and forth (accelerating and stopping). It's okay to have your rod tip perpendicular to the ground, or slightly elevated (not overhead). As you move the rod tip and let out more line, your strokes get longer and more deliberate. Do it right, and that fly line will go from twitching, to jumping, to gradually taking flight, almost like an albatross lifting off the ground.

4. It Helps to Keep Your Thumb in Your Peripheral Vision

It's an oldie but a great tip that solves more than half of novice fly-casting problems in one simple fix. As you grip the fly rod (most typically with your thumb on the top of the cork grip), have it in your mind that you want that thumb never to leave your peripheral vision. Don't look at your casting thumb; keep your eyes forward and on the target. But if you always have a sense of where that thumb is, you're going to solve the problems of a) going back too far on your backcast; and b) breaking your wrist too much as you cast. And those are the two most common problems associated with fly casting. (You might not think that by keeping your thumb in your peripheral vision, your rod tip is able to travel between 10 and 2 on the imaginary clock face, but trust us, that's exactly where it will be.)

If you keep your casting thumb in your peripheral vision, you won't go too far back, or break your wrist too much.

5. Your Backcast Is More Important Than Your Forward Cast

Well, not really. Your forward cast is always the delivery that matters the most. But, having said that, you cannot make a great delivery if you ignore the importance of the backcast. The backcast is where you generate all the energy and line speed. Think of it like this: the backcast is the engine, and the forward cast is the steering wheel.

Bahamian guide Torrie Bevins, who works the windy flats around South Andros, describes it as "rude boy . . . soft boy." Firm, with authority on the backcast. Stop the rod. Let the line extend, then gently steer it on target with the forward stroke.

That's particularly important when you cast into the wind. It's almost counterintuitive to go strong behind you, and easier forward, especially into the teeth of a breeze, but that's exactly how it works best.

6. It's Okay (Encouraged by Some) to Watch Your Loops

It's no secret what a good loop in a fly cast looks like. It's a traveling "U" shape (turned sideways). You want that U to be compact, like a wedge slicing through the air, but you don't want the line to double up and catch on itself (called a "tailing loop," that's usually caused by overpowering or overwristing the rod, particularly on that final-delivery, forward stroke). Likewise, you don't want that loop to look too loose and underdefined (called an "open loop," that's usually caused by not stopping the rod tip during the casting stroke, breaking the wrist, or going too far back or forward with the rod tip).

So here's the deal. Great, long loops overhead start with little loops near the ground. And if you can't first see good loops and know what they feel like as you make them, you won't be able to make them when you fish.

Practice short casts so you can see and feel "U" shapes form.

7

Another very useful exercise is to stand at the end of a dock on a lake, or out in the backyard, and run a piece of rope or a tape measure in a long, straight line in front of you. Now, tilting your rod sideways (parallel to the ground) start making short, crisp casts, and strive to make that perfect "U" shape with every flick. At first, it shouldn't be much more than exactly that—flicks of the wrist (remember to fling the tomato)—but eventually, they'll get longer and involve backcasts. Once you're stringing together 20- to 30-footers and forming that tight wedge, go ahead and lift the cast over your head and do it there. It's also okay (encouraged) to watch your loops form and travel as you are practice casting.

This exercise is one you never outgrow. Even the most seasoned casters in the world will take a little time to tune up on the basics and feel the loops form now and then.

7. Distance Doesn't Matter

Of course, it's fun to cast a fly line a long way. It takes incredible skill to be able to cast so far that you get a glimpse of your backing knot as it travels out the tip of the rod. That's something any angler might aspire to accomplish, and the more you can boom it, the more you inevitably enhance your casting prowess. And it's great fun to take part in casting competitions and all that.

But being able to cast far is not the price of admission to be a very skilled trout angler. Distance casting has almost no value whatsoever in 99.9 percent of most trout-fishing situations to be experienced anywhere on the planet.

Cast with your feet. Wade quietly into position for an accurate, 30-foot cast before you ever attempt to fire off some

70-foot hero shot with a dry fly (even if you get it there, odds are you won't be able to control the line well enough to make a clean presentation or set the hook if your fly gets hit). Granted, sometimes the river situation is such that you must cast for distance to reach spots where you can't wade through, but in trout fishing, a cast of more than 50 feet should either be a last resort or pure self-amusement.

If you want to be a deadly caster, in any fly-fishing scenario, from the trout river to the saltwater flats, practice the "40 feet in 4 seconds" drill. Set out three or four targets, 40 feet away from you. Then, from your stationary casting position, have a friend call out one of those targets. Starting by holding the fly in your hand, and having stripped out the necessary 40 feet of line needed to reach that target, you get 4 seconds (one Mississippi, two Mississippi . . .) to drop that fly right on the money.

Get so you can do that, more often than not, and you won't even process the nerves when you see that big brown trout grab a hopper by the riverbank.

8. We All Should Practice Roll Casting

So much attention is placed on the overhead fly cast, but when you really think about it, an effective angler can have a very productive day on most trout rivers without ever putting the line in the air (at least not much). The roll cast is extremely important for a number of reasons. First, false casts spook fish. If you're able to load the rod and fling line with a simple roll cast, you improve your chances of hookups. Second (and let's face it, we've all been there . . .), it's a heckuva lot harder to stick your fly in a tree behind you when you are roll casting, versus when you cast overhead.

So since we've already talked about how accurate short casts are more important than pretty long casts, why not take that next step and work on making those short casts by rolling your line?

There is one simple, important factor in making good roll casts. Start with your rod tip low. Just as you would on a regular cast, you want to accelerate into the casting motion. As you retrieve the line with a low rod tip, you create surface tension with the friction caused by the water surface and that loads the rod, just like a false cast would. Also, just as you would with a regular cast, you need to stop the rod tip at delivery. The roll cast isn't so much an "O" in shape as it is a "C."

The more comfortable you get with roll casting, the less fatigued you will feel at the end of a day of fishing. An efficient trout angler will make half of his casts during a given day by rolling . . . letting the moving water load the rod . . . and keeping that fly line out of the air, where it often causes trouble.

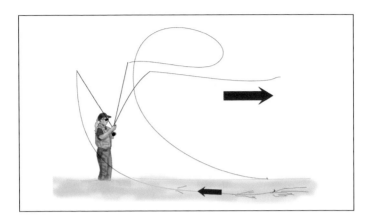

9. Your "Virtual Target" Is Really Above the Water Surface

Of course, the trout are in the water, and that's ultimately where you want your fly to land. But to make an effective cast, you need your full leader and tippet to unfurl above the water line, and then drop gracefully onto the surface.

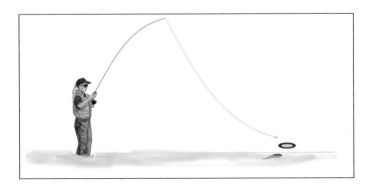

Don't get in the habit of banging your flies straight down on the water surface. Sometimes, practice casting into a hula hoop laying flat on the ground can be counterproductive for that very reason—it gets you so you are driving your flies at a downward angle. Remember, when you are standing in the water, you're a couple feet shorter than you are when you're standing in the yard casting at those hula hoops. It's often better to spend time practicing by casting into a garbage can, or a 5-gallon bucket, or something that's raised a little bit off the ground. That'll put your target where it really belongs: a little bit above the water surface.

10. Ugly Casts Catch Fish

A great fly cast is something to strive toward. It really is an art to make a fly line dance. For some people, that comes naturally; for others, the cast can be a reflection of years spent on the water, honing a skill. Aim to be the best you can be. Demand as much as you can from yourself. Practice, no matter how good you get, will never hurt you. A golfer doesn't expect to step on the first tee and drive the ball perfectly down the middle of the fairway without first having driven bucket after bucket of practice balls. It's unrealistic (and unfair, frankly) for any fly angler to expect instant gratification without having worked on their cast. That's not a fault of fly fishing; it's one of the most beautiful aspects of the sport.

That said, don't be intimidated by the learning curve. Embrace it. And understand that the beauty of this sport is that you get unlimited "mulligans." And nobody is keeping score, other than yourself.

So you punt that cast . . . who cares? The fish often don't. We've seen more huge trout caught after crummy casts than we can remember. And while we sometimes cheer for the trout, we always cheer for the angler who cares, wants to get better, and sometimes gets lucky. No pressure, people. This is all about fun. Never take that casting stuff too seriously. After all, there are other factors—like choosing flies, and reading water, and presenting your fly after it lands on the water—that matter way more than all the fancy loops and casts you might muster. We're going to dive into those things next.

Troubleshooting the Cast

Odds are, if you are like any other normal human being, as you learn to cast the fly rod, you are prone to make one of three mistakes. Here's what they are, and here's how you fix those problems.

You Go Too Far Back on the Backcast

You've been told "10 and 2." You think your arm is stopping exactly at 10 and 2 on that imaginary clock face. You're really going 10 and 3:30. You don't feel it, but it's happening. That's why you're throwing slushy, open loops when you cast, and the line dies and piles up in a frustrating clump in front of you.

The fix: Listen to what we said about the "thumb in the peripheral vision" thing. Stop the rod next to your ear on the backcast. Stop it with authority. Now shoot the line forward. Remember, that rod flexes, so if you stop the butt section at 12 o'clock, the tip is still traveling to 2 o'clock. Hammer forward. Load the rod with an aggressive backcast, but stop it shorter than you think you should. It's much easier to fix the caster who is driving tacks with an aggressive forward stroke than it is to fix and replace all the energy that's lost with a lazy backcast.

You Break Your Wrist Too Much as You Make the Cast

Your thumb shouldn't wiggle much more than a couple inches as you make that cast. Breaking your wrist too much immediately dissipates all the hard-earned energy you create in a normal casting stroke.

Simple fixes: Tuck the reel seat of your rod in your shirtsleeve. That will stop your wrist for you. Or put a rubber band on your wrist, and tuck the reel seat inside that. You'll feel the band flex when it's time to stop and stroke. Switch from having your thumb on the top side of the cork grip of your rod to placing your index finger along the top of the grip. Some of the best anglers the world has ever known—including the late, great Lee Wulff—made a living by casting that way.

Last, you want to take a lot of the loose arm motion out of your cast anyway. Practice by casting with a newspaper or magazine tucked in your armpit. Drop the prop, and you lose the cast. Keep it tight, compact, and most of the casting flaws will go away.

The Tailing Loop

You're simply trying too hard, captain. Take some of the sauce off that final, forward stroke. Hard back, easy forward. Don't snap that wrist. Trust your fly rod. If you set everything up correctly, the results will inevitably follow.

More Things You Should Know about Casting a Fly Rod

It's *Simply* about Loading the Rod . . .

None of the magic of our sport happens unless the fly gets in front of a fish. Casting is a critical and often frustrating skill to acquire, and most anglers, including myself, spend the rest of their lives improving this skill. But getting the basics together isn't as difficult as it may first seem, and mastering the cast isn't really necessary; most anglers will never get into the same time zone as "perfect," but they will still catch a lot of fish.

At the heart of the cast is loading the rod—getting the rod to bend under the weight of the fly line. Whenever I find my cast going awry, it's usually because I'm not getting a good bend in the rod during my casting stroke. In those moments I go back to the basics: 1) start with the rod tip close to the water—the more of your fly line that is connected to the water, the better the load; 2) start with no more than 10 to 15 feet of fly line out—just enough to bend the rod, not so much that it's unmanageable; 3) make sure your stops at each end of the casting stroke are abrupt; 4) watch your backcast—yes, turn your head and watch it, make sure the fly line straightens out and fully loads the rod before you start your forward stroke; and 5) add a little single haul on the backcast to increase line speed and load the rod faster (the secret sauce that I picked up by watching really good casters).

—Steve Zakur, Connecticut

Rifle Shoot That Cast

When prospecting for trout, don't flock shoot and cast to the top of the run where you think there might be a fish and let your fly drift through the whole run. Split the pool or run into thirds or halves. Cast to the water in front of you first and then move up. The other way will have you catching only one fish and spooking the rest with drag or lining the fish. Similarly, only cast the length of the leader or less so there is no impact on the fish from your line hitting the water. Doing this will also let you have a drag-free drift of your fly.

—Alice Owsley, Riverside Anglers,
West Yellowstone, Montana

The Mirror Effect

Just like it's always shocking to hear your own voice, it can also be surprising to see what you look like when you cast. There's a reason ballet studios and music rooms have large mirrors: this is the way you see and correct mistakes. It's not only that artist-types are narcissists. So set up a tripod or get a friend to film you (every phone nowadays has a video option). If you sincerely want to improve, have that same friend view the footage with you, analyzing form and identifying what might be holding accuracy or distance back. Then take that constructive criticism, fix what was broken, and get back out on the water. Better this time.

—Erin Block, Boulder, Colorado

The Basic Ingredients Needed to Develop an Effective Casting Stroke

Fly fishing should be a simple, enjoyable pastime. That includes learning a basic casting stroke and honing it over time to improve your skills. Yet time and again, I see many people who are teaching others the basics of casting overcomplicate this process. Fly casting, as with most things in life, is best kept simple.

Start with the grip. Take hold of the fly-rod handle as if you were shaking someone else's hand. Grip it lightly, with the same amount of pressure that you would use if you were holding an uncooked egg. Remember, your entire rig including rod, reel, backing, fly line, leader, tippet, and flies usually weighs just slightly more than one-half pound. You certainly don't need much grip pressure to control something as light as that.

The basic casting stroke itself is very much like driving a long nail into an imaginary vertical board that is just in front of you. You start driving a nail by holding the hammer in a vertical position, where your hand is close to your ear. In driving a nail, it is natural to keep your elbow close to your side, not extended out as if you were throwing a baseball. The same goes with fly casting. Since your elbow is at your side, this means that the casting stroke is mostly done with the forearm. The part of your arm from your elbow to your shoulder has very little to do with the process. When starting the hammer in the vertical position, your natural tendency is to cock your wrist to the rear ever so slightly. This wrist cock is almost imperceptible, but it is there.

The next motion in hammering the nail is to bring the hammer forward by moving your entire forearm toward the imaginary board. While you may not think about it, this motion is a slow acceleration to a sudden stop just before you release the hammerhead toward the nail. Again, your elbow is close to your side, and the very slight wrist cock you had in the vertical position is maintained during the forward stroke.

As your forearm approaches the imagined vertical board, it comes to a sudden stop. At that time, you release the slight wrist cock that you established at the start of the stroke when the hammer was in the vertical position. This enables you to figuratively throw the hammerhead into the nail.

During this process your arm starts in roughly a vertical position and finishes at about a 45-degree angle to both the imaginary wall and the surface you are standing on. You should avoid making your casting motion too long. You do not want to reach way back past the vertical position that you established at the start of the cast or follow all the way through to a horizontal position at the end of the forward stroke. Remember, you are trying to emulate the way that you drive a nail, not the way you throw a baseball. In the basic fly cast, the forearm never moves much more than 45 degrees from the vertical during the stroke.

It is the gradual acceleration to a sudden stop that propels the fly line when casting. The concept is to put enough speed into the casting motion to make the rod tip bend during the slow acceleration to a sudden stop on both the forward and the backward cast. When you come to a sudden stop at the end of the stroke, this causes the bent fly rod to straighten. That straightening is what imparts the energy in the fly rod into the fly line, hurtling it out.

Casting a fly rod is not a process where you use your strength to propel the fly line, as you would when throwing a baseball. Instead, it is similar to the way that you use the momentum of a jump rope to circle it around the jumper. Trying to muscle the rod and the line by imparting too much force is a common mistake and a source of frustration with those who don't understand the concept of the slow acceleration to a sudden stop.

The last basic that you need to remember is that you have to let your fly line completely straighten out before you change directions with your casting stroke whether you are going forward or backward. That is, on your backcast, you must pause long enough to let the line straighten out behind you before you start the rod forward. Similarly, if you intend to false cast back and forth, you must let the line straighten out in front of you before starting the rod back. The more line you have off of the end of the rod tip, the longer you must wait before changing directions with the rod. This is best learned by actually turning around while you are casting so that you can see the line straighten on both the backcast and the forward cast.

You can practice your fly casting even when you are not fishing. Often when I am driving, I practice by making a motion like driving a nail into an imaginary vertical board in front of me. I start with my arm in a vertical position with a slight wrist cock and make a slow acceleration forward to a sudden stop, uncocking my wrist at the very end of the forward stroke. I then repeat these steps in reverse while practicing my backcast. Repeating the words "back . . . pause . . . forward . . . pause" helps me visualize the idea of starting the imaginary hammer in the vertical position and moving it forward with my forearm to the imaginary nail in front of me. Try it; it really does work, and it is a way to surreptitiously spend time fishing even when you are not on the water.

There is a lot to learn about fly casting, and these concepts certainly aren't all that you will need to know. However, if you are working on the fundamentals of fly fishing, or if you are having some problems with your current casting, you might want to consider the concept of driving a nail into an imaginary vertical board to help you keep things simple and lay down a solid base for more advanced techniques.

—John Gray

Practice and Conditioning Are Key

To enjoy fly fishing, the following tips have proven to be extremely helpful and true: take the time to learn how to cast and practice, practice, and practice. Practice is not for the day you go fly fishing! Similarly, take the time to get into shape so you can get to that great spot and be able to fish it all day.

—Gary Hogue, Northwestern Carolina Chapter

Women Are Naturally Better

I am a retired former owner of a fly shop in the upper Midwest. During the course of the 11 years I owned the shop, I conducted many fly-casting classes and clinics for the beginner flyfisherperson.

The main observation I always made while conducting these classes is that beginning women students generally caught on to the program better and quicker than the beginning men. Why? Two reasons: women don't overpower the rod like men seem to do, and women listen to instructions better than men.

I have voiced this observation to other shop owners who conducted similar classes and received almost unanimous agreement. Our conclusion is this . . . Guys, leave your muscles in the gym, fly casting is not a strength sport, and listen to your instructor. He or she just may know what they are talking about.

—Mac Richardson, Cheboygan, Michigan

A Good Cast Is One That Gets Your Fly Wet

I'd like to pass along a tip I received many years ago when I was new to fly fishing. This tidbit of valuable information came from an experienced angler and fellow teacher one evening on the Shenandoah River. After about a half hour of trying to impress my older friend with my casting skills (double-haul, roll cast, turn my head to check my back cast, you name it), he looked at me and said, "Try to keep your line in the water as much as possible. That's where the fish are." Best tip I ever got.

—Chuck Way, Front Royal, Virginia

Master the Curve Cast

The curve cast is a good trick to have in the arsenal, especially when you want to drop a dry fly in a specific spot but a boulder or overhanging tree branch blocks the straight line between you and your target. It also works where heavy currents or obstacles make a downstream presentation impractical.

Some people call it a hinge cast, because the premise is to power the fly line, then stop the rod tip (and the line) abruptly so the leader swings around and kicks the fly to the side.

- Get within 20 to 50 feet of your target. As you start casting, move the plane of your rod from straight overhead to 45 degrees—or even sidearm—so the path of your line is nearly parallel to the water surface.
- Accelerate the forward cast to generate line speed, but stop the rod abruptly as the line straightens. When the line is almost fully extended, flick your wrist so the reel actually points in the direction you want your fly to land.

- Stop the line with the index finger of your casting hand, or by pulling taut with your line hand if you're double hauling. As you see the leader cock sideways, drop the rod tip and let your fly fall gently to the surface.

—Kirk Deeter (K. D.)

Three Tricks to Tame the Wind

Sometimes you must be able to punch through a stiff breeze to get your fly in front of fish. Here are three key casting tips that can help you do just that:

1. Your thumb should be way at the top edge of the rod grip, almost touching the graphite. So choke up on the grip and really accentuate the power in your thumb.
2. Use the headwind to your advantage by generating line speed to load the rod on your backcast. Back with authority, forward with grace. That may seem counterintuitive, because

The key to casting in wind is forming a tight loop.

you want to punch into the wind, but the power move is really the backcast.

3. Tip three has to do with gear. Your line choice is 100 times more important than your rod's design when it comes to casting into the wind. You can never buy your way to an effective wind cast; only practice develops that. But the line is the key ingredient in all this, and lines are a lot less expensive than rods.

—K. D.

Focus on Your Line Selection as Much as Your Rod Selection

Along those same ... um ... lines, when I consider the amount of time and energy devoted by hunters to topics like cartridges for rifles, or shells for shotguns, or arrows for bows, I cannot help but wonder why so few fly anglers carefully consider the line they use.

If anglers thought half as much about what line to use on their 5-weight as a shooter does about whether to fire 165-grain or 180-grain bullets through a 30.06, most questions

about how to effectively cast would answer themselves. And a good fly line can make a budget rod seem like it can perform miracles, while conversely, a shoddy line will knock the performance straight out of the most expensive rod.

It's one thing to decide whether you want a double-taper (say, for delicate dry-fly presentations) or a weight-forward line (a good all-around option), or a sink tip (for fishing streamers)—that's the easy part. But even if you are looking at the most common line (the WF5F), it's important to realize that all options are not alike. Different elements, such as coatings, core materials, and surface textures, all matter, and the line makers guard their manufacturing processes like you wouldn't believe.

That said, one aspect of fly lines always in plain sight is taper design. Fly lines are different than the monofilament, braid, or fluorocarbon used with conventional tackle in that they're weighted. The weight of the line is what the angler leverages to hurl a very light fly, and the weight rating of a line, in general, is meant to correspond to the size rod it's paired with. But where that weight is distributed in a line can make a huge difference when it comes to casting and fishing. For example, a line with all its weight packed near the front is going to generate energy to chuck flies, but a distance caster is going to want some weight reserved for the middle section; otherwise, you'll have to strip in all the belly, and then shoot on every cast to generate any length. Mending is critically important to an effective presentation, and some lines mend better than others. Again, if all the weight is bunched up like a bullet in the front of the line, and all you have to lift and move is running line, you won't be able to mend as effectively as you would with some weight distributed farther back. If I'm turning over big streamers and making repeat casts at moderate or short distances (like banging the banks from a drift boat), I want that weight packed up front so I can lift and fire at will. On the other hand, double tapers work well for dry-fly fishing with rods that are 4-weights or lighter, in particular. For most fiberglass rods, I still like weight-forward lines, but that's just me.

It's okay to go "off-label," too, but before you start "over-lining" rods, realize that a number of very popular lines are already weighted one-half to one full weight more than the rod they're supposedly made for. And some lines might say that they are made for a certain situation (and they well may be), but they certainly aren't limited to that particular use. For example, I've found that some lines marketed for roll casting are actually some of the very best for forming tight overhead loops, provided your fishing is concentrated within 50 feet or so (where it should be on a trout river). A great roll-casting line can be an even better overhead casting line if you let it.

Of course, everybody's casting style and fishing interests are different, so I'm urging you to play around a bit, and hone in on the taper that's right for you. Try some options your friends have that you don't. Or most respectable fly shops will let you test cast different lines before you buy one. You should try different lines with at least the same diligence as you would test cast rods before buying one.

Trust me, I'm not falling for the marketing hype and saying that you need a different line for every situation you fish. I am saying, though, that there are legitimate differences in line tapers, and that the more you learn about them and match the right line to your own style and interests, the better you will cast and the better you will fish. Plus, you could even save yourself money if you currently think that a new rod, rather than a new line, will solve your casting woes.

—K. D.

Casting in the Dark Improves Your Feel and Timing

A good friend and I once put on a fairly placid section of the Colorado River at 7 p.m., and we floated until almost 1 a.m. It was a section I know like the back of my hand, and it barely has any real obstacles to maneuver around. That said, we did bring some very powerful headlamps and flashlights as back-up. The objective was to throw large streamers and mice patterns for anything that might eat them. Namely, very large brown trout.

Unfortunately for us, the night turned much, much colder than the weatherman had predicted or than we had anticipated, and basically shut the fishing down.

Undaunted, we cast and cast and cast again. For hours and hours, with really nothing to show for it. We lost some bugs and dealt with a few tangles, but the next morning waiting for coffee to brew, we both came to the conclusion that casting all night in the pitch black actually helped our skills out and maybe we should do it more often. It sounds strange, but you learn to "feel" takes, the bank, bushes, and current lines much better than if you were simply fishing during the day. While you're definitely not as accurate, I do think you end up losing fewer bugs after gaining that sense of touch that you can only acquire at night. It's tough to describe, but I think we both felt at a certain point that we knew exactly how far to cast, even though we could barely see the bank. When to mend, even though we couldn't see eddy lines. We just felt a lot more "in tune" with our lines and rods.

—Tim Romano, Boulder, Colorado

Nudge a Bad Cast, but Don't Rip It Away

If your cast is a little off target, continue to work the fly so as not to "spook" the trout in the water where they may be holding. You might pick up one where you thought there were none.

—Dan Beistel, Oviedo, Florida

How to Generate More Line Speed

The trick to casting a fly rod well is generating line speed. That not only adds distance to your cast, but also, with the fast action / quick recovery rods most anglers use these days, line speed is key to accuracy. If you're not generating line speed, you simply aren't using a fly rod to full effect.

Generating line speed is key to a good fly cast.

It's a pretty simple deal if you focus on three simple things:

1. Start the backcast with the rod tip low to the water. Doing so uses the surface tension from the water to flex and load the fly rod. If you start the cast with the tip high, you have less leverage.
2. Accelerate and stop. Build into the backcast, but stop the rod high. If you don't stop the rod, you let all the energy of your cast pour out the back. Think of it like you're lifting a glass of water off a table, and throwing it over your shoulder.
3. Haul. Pull on the line with your non-casting hand as you make your false casts. Many novice anglers are intimidated by the idea of double hauling, but it doesn't have to be complicated. Even tugging the line a few inches with your fingertips will boost line speed. You don't need to haul in bunches; a little bit will help you develop the timing.

—K. D.

Cast the Amount of Line You Can Handle, and You Cast Well

Beware of having too much line out, and beware of thrashing the water with your casts. You naturally want to be gentle with putting the fly in front of your fish. It's easy to scare away a nice big rainbow or brown with a clunky presentation. The lesson is, it's far better to work with a measure of line that you can cast accurately and land gently than too much line that is hard to aim, hard to control, hard to mend after it hits the water, and makes too much noise when it does.

—Susie W. Leeson, Steamboat Springs, Colorado

The "haul" is a simple tug of the fly line with your off hand as your cast goes forward.

Give It a Go!

Why not cast? Often we blast past marginal-looking water to get to spots that are obviously fishy. Why not try a cast or two? Again, it's amazing the kind of spots that can hold good fish. Case in point: A few years ago on Alaska's Chena River, I saw a tiny pool that obviously didn't have a fish in it. I was getting ready to walk upstream when up comes an 18-inch grayling, appearing from nowhere. Happens all the time on little trout streams here in the East. They don't always produce fish, but if not I wasted 8 seconds on a cast. Oh well.

—Mark Taylor, Roanoke, Virginia

A Longer Rod Makes for a Better Bow-and-Arrow Cast

On tiny water (like we have so much of here in the East), a lot of folks want to go to these really short rods. When it gets really tight, it can be better to go (kind of) long. An 8-footish rod allows for casting when there is some room but is much more effective for the bow-and-arrow casts that are absolutely critical.

—Mark Taylor

Play Your "Ace" Cast First

I think the odds of catching a fish diminish proportionately with every cast you make, even if you switch flies in between casts. So you want to make the first one count. One well-conceived, well-placed cast is worth one thousand blind casts where you're spraying it all over the place, even when you are not sight fishing or fishing to a rising trout. You want to have a pinpoint target in mind, and then hit it. The first time. If you take a moment to visualize what you want to do, you'll often do

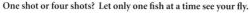

One shot or four shots? Let only one fish at a time see your fly.

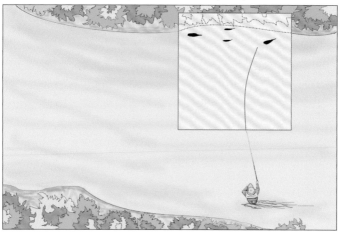

it. Just like visualizing the golf shot you want to make, or the free throw you want to sink.

—Sarah Deeter, Pine, Colorado

Pick a Specific Target

When casting, pick out a specific target rather than just cast in a general direction. Pick out a spot at a confluence point, along structure, above a riffle, along a seam, along the riverbank or in "open" water. Other targets may include "nervous" water, a foam line, bubbles, a dark spot, and so on. This will result in a better cast.

—Dan Beistel

Keep False Casts Off-Target

False casts are free, and they're great for helping you measure out and judge distance. But they also spook fish. Several years

Stalking and spotting fish from well out of the water, New Zealand style.

ago, I stopped false casting directly over my target and started moving my false casts a little bit to the side, maybe only 3 or 4 feet. Only the final delivery goes right over the trout. My percentage of takes has gone up dramatically.

—Sarah Deeter

Hunt for the Trout of a Lifetime: Walk, Spot, Stalk . . . and THEN Cast

Too many anglers waste precious time blind casting hoping to hook fish. Fishing for the trophy fish is much like hunting big

game. The dedicated big-game hunter walks, spots, stalks, and shoots; of course, you don't shoot (perhaps line), but the ritual is the same if you want success on the stream. Anyway, the more you walk, the farther you will find yourself "away from the annoying crowds."

—Conway Bowman, Encinitas, California

No Pressure! Remember What You're Really Fishing For

Enjoy the moment. Most important, when we forget it is fishing, to have fun and enjoy, we miss the point. You never know when or if you may be in this river with your fishing buddy watching brookies rise to tricos with mad passion like the time before. Relish every moment.

—Brian Kozminski,
Boyne City, Michigan

One Simple Move, One Simple Bug

If you can roll cast and know how to swing a soft hackle, you may not catch every fish in the stream, but you will always be in the game.

—Greg Potter

Keep in Touch with That Line

With my clients, I find that many of them lose touch with their fly line following their cast. I emphasize holding on to their line throughout the cast with their line hand, and then transferring their line to their rod hand and tucking it under their index finger to maintain "contact" with their fly.

This allows them to be ready to strike immediately following their cast, and they are not looking and fumbling for their line—instead, they are able to concentrate on their fly, and it allows them to strip through their rod hand either as they mend their fly or following hookup.

—Guide Larry Lewis, Dubois, Wyoming

Keep Counting

When casting a dry or streamer, count "1, 2, 3" with your rod ending at 12 o'clock, then "1, 2, 3" again for the cast. My daughter was making beautiful loops in 15 minutes her first time at Lovell's on the Au Sable in Michigan by doing just that.

—Bob Gorski, Grosse Pointe, Michigan

Try Tenkara

My tip? Try tenkara. Tenkara is the Japanese method of fly fishing using only a long telescoping rod, a line with 3 to 6 feet of tippet, and a fly. The rod is 10 to 15 feet in length, and the line is usually the length of the rod. The hackle on the fly is often reversed—facing forward over the hook eye. In tenkara fly fishing, the emphasis is on presentation—"the fly does not matter"—while in Western angling, the focus is more about fly selection—"matching the hatch"—and less on presentation. Tenkara is an excellent way to introduce beginning anglers to the sport of fly fishing, as it has fewer accoutrements than Western-style fly fishing. There is no reel and accompanying line handling to befuddle the neophyte; no strike indicator, no split shot, and no floatant. The cost is considerably less than a Western outfit.

With apologies to David Letterman, here are my top 10 reasons you should give tenkara a try:

10. **Minimal gear.** Necessary to catch fish–a rod, line, tippet, and fly.

9. **Effective.** In Japan, tenkara is said to outfish Western gear in small mountain streams. This statement may or may not be true, but from my experience, I'm certainly not catching any fewer fish than I did fishing Western style.

8. **The long rod.** Reaches across currents, allowing long drag-free drifts, it requires no line mending, and can drop a fly in front of a fish, making a delicate presentation that can't be easily accomplished with Western tackle.

7. **Stalking fish.** Anglers are able to get close to the fish. The long rod and nearly invisible line don't alarm the fish.

6. **Sensitivity.** The rod, line, and fly are directly connected to the angler transmitting the feel of the fly in the water. And when a fish is hooked, a small fish feels like a large fish does on stiffer Western tackle.

5. **Ultralight weight.** Makes it ideal for backpacking and hiking. An entire kit can weigh as little as 5 or 6 ounces, including rod, line, line holder, tippet spool, and flies.

4. **Portability.** The rod collapses down to 20 or so inches in length and requires no protective tube, as the small, more delicate tip sections are protected by the heavier butt sections.

3. **Easy to do, a lifetime to master.** Tenkara is easily learned because the focus is on technique and presentation, not on equipment. Beginners can quickly get into fish. It also presents a continuing challenge to veteran anglers—mastering presentation techniques and then determining which technique will entice the fish on any particular day or water.

2. **Specialized small-stream angling.** Arguably, this is the best method for fly fishing small streams.
1. **FUN.** Catching fish on tenkara has proven to be the most enjoyable means of fly fishing. So much so, that my wife and I have almost totally abandoned Western angling. We only resort to Western angling when tenkara tools and techniques are not suitable.

Give tenkara a try; you will be glad you did.

—Mark Cole, PhD, Leadville, Colorado

Remember These Words . . .

For many years, I have been using just two words when discussing fly fishing. Those two words are "always enjoy"! Plus those two words go beyond fly fishing and should also apply to everything every day. Nobody will ever regret it!

Joe Humphreys, fly-fishing legend, gave an interesting suggestion at our local TU chapter when he said, "Don't forget to look up and around while you are fishing." Good advice, indeed.

—Sherwin Albert Jr, Milton, Pennsylvania

CHAPTER 2

10 Things You Should Know about Fly Selection

1. The Key Is Knowing When Trout Want to Eat Something Specific, versus When You Must Tease a Bite

In its oldest, purest form, fly fishing is about "matching the hatch." You create a fly that looks like natural insects, which trout eat. You show that fly to the fish, and, mistaking it as a natural bug, the trout eats the fly. Simple, right? Hardly. Matching bugs to fish can be one of the most complex and challenging—yet ultimately rewarding—aspects of the sport.

But before you start matching hatches, it's important to watch the fish and the river, to know if they are keyed into a specific hatch in the first place. When you see rise rings, and trout noses, and clouds of insects flying around, you just need to grab one of those natural insects and find a fly in your box that looks like it.

But if there are no rise forms, and no naturals, you're going to have to make them an offer they cannot refuse. And that means an attractor of some sort. Big and ugly, bright and gaudy works as an attractor, while subtle and muted, exact and honest works when you match the hatch.

Two different games. The trick is knowing exactly which game you are playing, run by run, minute by minute.

2. The Hardest Puzzle to Solve: When Trout Have a Lot of Choices

So what happens when you see fish working, either on the surface, or below (you know they are eating by how they move), but there are many insect options to choose from? You see skittering caddis, and emerging mayflies, maybe some midges . . . and a grasshopper just jumped into the river, too. In those situations, I like to give them the biggest, easiest meal and size down from there. But if I am wrong the first time, I switch that fly, right then.

3. A Fly on the Water Is Worth Two in the Hand

Some flies are meant to catch fish, and some flies are meant to catch anglers. I am always surprised by how some of the patterns I think are surefire winners because they look so snazzy just turn out to be duds. And sometimes, the plainest, ugliest fly I tied myself turns out to be the belle of the ball. And sometimes, the rattier a fly is, after it gets chewed on a few times, the better it works. Remember this: how a fly looks to a fish from the water is a thousand times more important than how a fly looks to you as you hold it in your hand.

4. Profile Matters Most

There are many factors that influence what a fish likes or doesn't like about a fly—especially when you are matching naturals. Color . . . size . . . profile . . . materials (action), etc.: all matter to varying degrees. But if I had to pick the most important factors, I'd start with size and profile. How closely does the fly match the natural bugs in terms of size and general (very general, sometimes) shape? If you're a tick off on color shade, and you have a big white calf-tail post but from the bottom looking up, the fly is just about that right shape and size, you're going to be in the game. Which is why the Parachute Adams is the best do-anything dry-fly pattern in the history of the world, in my humble opinion.

5. Vulnerability Is an Asset (for a Fly)

When fish have lots of options in terms of the number of bugs in or on the water, I always skew toward using a more vulnerable pattern, oftentimes a cripple or an emerger. For example, during a blanket Callibaetis hatch on the Madison Arm of Hebgen Lake, Montana, I couldn't buy a bite, even though I was throwing a trustworthy dry-fly pattern into working trout. Only when I switched to the cripple, which looks like a fly that just cannot quite get out of its shuck, straighten up, and fly right . . . did I find the bite. Make it easy on the fish, and you will make it easy on yourself.

6. Size Down or Switch on a Refusal

If you know a fish saw your fly and didn't pay attention to it, switch your pattern entirely. When the fish does pay attention, maybe even tracks it . . . rises . . . juuuuust about opens

Smaller, no-frills patterns are often a safe bet.

its mouth, but, at the last minute, says, "Nah, thanks anyway," you also want to switch and wait a bit before the next cast. But that switch should be to the same pattern fly (or close), one size smaller. You almost sealed the deal with a 16. I'd hit 'em with an 18 next time. Doesn't always work, but it works better than sizing larger, or making a blind guess at another pattern.

7. Never Underestimate the Value of Midges

More than 50 percent of a trout's food, in most places in North America, is comprised of midges—those tiny bugs that are seemingly everywhere. Some of us don't like fishing patterns that small, but remember that midges cluster, thus the relevance of the Griffith's Gnat, or the Grizzly Cluster. I've even thrown a size 14 Blue Dun into a midge hatch, let the natural bugs take a ride, and ultimately fed a big brown trout a midge meatball. And unless you are working subsurface midge patterns like the Black Beauty, at least once in a while, you really aren't in the game.

8. The Best Flies Can Be Fished in More Ways Than One

Rather than having 100 flies to fish in 100 different scenarios, it might be better, and more cost effective, to have 10 flies that can be fished in 10 different ways. Why do you think the Muddler Minnow is so popular? Because it's a grasshopper as well as a minnow. Woolly Bugger? A leech, maybe a baitfish, who knows what else? You can use your nippers or scissors to make small adjustments—cut down that wing to make the fly ride lower. Pull out a Sharpie pen to turn that light fly dark. There are no rules against being innovative in fly fishing . . . only rewards for being so.

9. Colors Change in Water

Do you ever wonder why a purple Prince Nymph works, even though there are no purple bugs that look exactly like that, anywhere? It's because trout do see colors, and they are more perceptive to the violet side of the spectrum. Part of that also has to do with the fact that red turns to gray as light is absorbed the deeper one goes in water. Red actually looks gray 10 feet under the water (that's why you often need to add a red filter when photographing under water). On the surface, with dry flies, you can't go wrong by being as natural as possible—or as "standout" as possible with an attractor. But depending on how deep you are fishing nymphs, matching colors to match exact bugs may not be a big deal, and you might want to skew more toward an attention grabber, with the right profile.

10. Flies I Never Leave Home Without

Black Woolly Bugger. Muddler Minnow. Parachute Adams. Elk Hair Caddis. Dave's Hopper. Mole Fly (Craven). Prince Nymph. Pheasant Tail Nymph. Copper John Nymph. Black Zebra Midge.

The Muddler Minnow is one of the most versatile flies ever created.

Dave Whitlock Explains Classic Flies (Dries, Nymphs, and Streamers—reprinted from *Trout* magazine)

The Traditional Dry Fly

Since its conception in the 1800s, the dry fly has been an important mainstay in most every trout fisher's fly box. It may be that beautiful, aquatic mayfly adults—most likely *Ephemera danica*—floating like delicate sailboats on the smooth surface of English chalk streams inspired man to first fly fish for trout. The design, effectiveness, grace, beauty, and charm of these flies have captured the devotion of fly-fishing writers, poets, artists, and fly tiers throughout the centuries. I was so moved when I first witnessed this *danica* emergence on the Itchen in Hampshire, England. The experience of seeing a trout rise to the surface and capture a mayfly, and then rise again to an imitation of the mayfly you've just presented is a moving experience that is seldom forgotten and addictive to the degree that some trout flyfishermen never fish any other way again.

Just as the basic definition of a wet fly is a fly that sinks *into* the water, the dry fly is a fly that floats *on* water. Actually, most dry flies are captured in the water surface film leaving some or most of the fly extended above the surface. My references suggest that the traditional dry fly was originally created to imitate duns and spinners of *Ephemera*—the mayfly—by Frederick Halford, who lived in England in the late 1800s. After the traditional dry fly was well established in Europe, Theodore Gordon, an American enamored with Halford's work, began tying and then fishing these flies in the Catskills and other

northeastern trout waters in around 1889. American fly-fishing historians affectionately honor Mr. Gordon with the esteemed title of "Father of the American Dry Fly," and his Quill Gordon is most symbolic of the traditional dry fly in North America.

These early dry flies, on both continents, were considered practical only on calm, slow-moving chalk streams, spring creeks, and still waters. But after Emlyn Gill wrote *Practical Dry Fly Fishing* in 1912, followed by George LaBranche's *The Dry Fly and Fast Water* in 1914, the fly's acceptance on our faster-flowing trout streams began and has continued in popularity and design development ever since.

Here in the United States, traditional dry flies are often known as "Catskill" dry flies. Delicate and beautiful, they are designed and constructed to alight softly on the surface film and to rest upright and mostly above the surface as does the mayfly dun that it most frequently imitates. To achieve this performance, it is tied on a small, very light wire hook with extra fine silk or nylon thread, using the finest-sized cock hackle, duck-wing feather segments, duck breast or flank feathers, herl, hackle stems, and water-animal fur. To create perfect balance, the wings, hackle, thorax, body, tails, and heads call for very stringent proportions, and little or no cement is used. The most important imitative characteristics of the traditional dry fly are the wings, then thorax, abdomen, legs, and lastly the tail. This priority was established from observation of what was thought a trout sees from its underwater–eye view of mayfly duns and spinners on the surface as they float into the window of the trout's vision. The order of importance for choosing and fishing the fly was then thought to be size, presentation, color, form, buoyancy, and transparency.

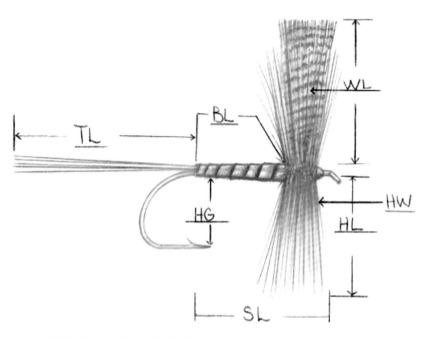

Whitlock's proportions for the classic dry fly.
Tail Length (TL)=Shank Length (SL)
Body Length (BL)=⅔ SL
Hackle Length (HL)=1½ Hook Gap (HG)
Wing Length (WL)=1¼ Hackle Length (HL)
HW=Hackle Width

The hypothetical *perfect* float position of the traditional dry fly is seldom, if ever, achieved because of the fly's connection to the line and leader, the way it is tied, the presentation, the condition of the water surface, and how well it actually floats. The hook and hackle barbules often protrude well below the surface in an unnatural manner. Yet trout, wild and tame, eagerly take this less-than-perfect imitation if presented with an acceptable size, color, and good drift. Discussions among flyfishermen and tiers on why this is so are wonderfully thought provoking. My own observation is that trout display a different rise action to the

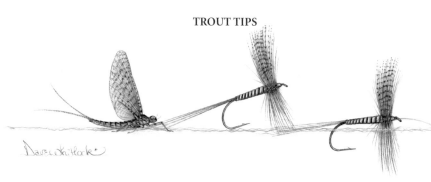

traditional dry fly than they do to the naturals, which seems to imply that, in the trout's opinion, the variations are acceptable within their opportunistic feeding drive and limited reasoning.

The traditional dry-fly patterns mostly reflect the general color and marking patterns of the mayfly hatches indigenous to the waters being fished, or, as Ernest Schwiebert coined it, "matching the hatch," in his book of the same title published in 1955. These patterns are mostly duns (gray), sulphurs (pale yellows), and olives. The attractor traditional dry flies, such as the Royal Coachman, were seldom as popular among the Catskill dry-fly purists.

If you'd like to know more about traditional dry flies and how to tie the classic patterns, I'd recommend the following: Ray Bergman's *Trout*, Edison Leonard's *Flies*, Darrel Martin's *The Fly Fisher's Craft*, Art Flick's *Streamside Guide*, and Ernest Schwiebert's *Matching the Hatch*. Each of these provides a special historic viewpoint of the traditional dry fly.

The traditional dry fly is still popular today, especially in our Eastern streams and still waters. The good news for this design is that we are constantly improving on the hooks, threads, and tying materials, especially the extra-high quality genetic cock hackle. The high-floating fly lines, tapered leader designs, and wonderful rods available today also enable us to be more successful at casting, presenting, drifting, and catching with these delicate flies. There are usually assortments of traditional dry flies available in fly shops and website stores. However, there truly is a magic to finding just the right materials and fine hooks and correctly tying to proportion these historic dry flies, and then tempting a beautiful trout to the surface. It's one of those incredibly fulfilling experiences in trout fly fishing. Give it a try.

Dave Whitlock

The Trout Fisher's Nymph

The nymph fly was originally considered an imitation of the immature phase of *Ephemeroptera* (mayflies). Developed in Europe during the late 1800s and early 1900s, G. E. M. Skues is most credited with the first impressionistic nymphal flies and the initial methods of fishing them for trout in England's southern chalk and limestone streams. Skues's observations of feeding trout and study of their stomach contents led him to correctly believe that trout feed most consistently on subsurface food forms day to day, month to month, and season to season. Many decades later, this method would eventually replace surface fly fishing for trout in popularity and effectiveness both on the European continent and in the United States. It's often said the Skues's first nymph book, *Minor Tactics for Trout,* should be retitled *Major Tactics.*

Although Skues's work received the most recognition, others in that period were contributing to the development of imitating subsurface insects and invertebrates. A "Dr. Bell" was paralleling Skues's line of reasoning on English stillwaters, but Bell was imitating immature chironomids (midges) and sedges (caddis flies). Bell developed the midge emerger "Bell's Buzzer" and the caddis emerger known as the "Amber Nymph."

Skues and the nymphing method he developed came under much criticism from the many dry-fly purists who believed that fishing a fly below the surface was almost sacrilege, especially from those privileged few who were members of exclusive fly-fishing clubs or royalty-owned chalk streams. The fly-fishing literature then and in the twentieth century has humorous and not-so-humorous stories about flyfishermen who were caught fishing below the surface on these sacred dry-fly waters. Even today, such subsurface trout flies are restricted on certain private trout waters.

Skues and one of his most respected nymph-fly disciples, Frank Sawyer, believed that only the abundant, swimming mayfly nymphs found in chalk streams were practical to imitate. As you can see in my illustrations, Skues's and Sawyer's favorite nymph patterns were *very* simple, impressionistic designs. When these flies and the nymphing technique came to America, they were unpopular and relatively ineffective because our trout waters (especially in the East) consist of streams that are very different from the English chalk streams. Likewise, these nymph flies were not good imitations of the varieties of burrowing and crawling mayflies, stoneflies, and other aquatic insects that occur in our freestone streams. The American nymph hybridization of the first European nymphs, along with a limited knowledge of the structure, texture, and living modes of the various important species, produced a series of nymphal designs that were quite unrealistic. I've included illustrations from some of the early American tiers: Hewitt, Burke, and Bergman. The result was a period of nymphal imitation limbo until the mid-twentieth century, when improving entomological knowledge of aquatic insects began to inspire such notable angler-tiers as Art Flick, Polly Rosborough, Al Troth, George Grant, John Atherton, Al McClane, Ted Trueblood, Doug Prince, Doug Swisher, Carl Richards, Al Caucci, Randall Kaufmann, Bob Nastasi, André Puyans, myself, and others, to create imitations that looked, felt, and fished like the major, nymphal aquatic insects across North America. Nymphing here also became easier and more popular after I developed and wrote about the strike indicator.

The successful nymph flies of this time had several things in common: they were impressionistic and had the correct sizes, color patterns, and densities to attract trout in streams throughout North and South America. Many of these flies were, and continue to be, extremely successful at enticing trout. Early on, most were mayfly and stonefly imitations. Caddis and midges, which are sometimes referred to as nymphs, have a larva and pupa stage instead of a nymphal form and so were not considered for imitating by most.

Although modern fly-tying materials and techniques allow tiers to sculpture nymph imitations that look precisely like the live forms, these beautiful, time-consuming imitations are often not as effective at catching trout. Just last summer, I tested some of the most realistic stonefly nymphs I'd ever seen, along with my favorite impressionistic stonefly nymphs, on the Madison and Yellowstone Rivers. My success ratio was always better when using the impressionistic imitations.

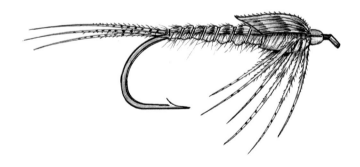

As I see it, there are three generations of nymph flies: those very sparsely tied, impressionistic nymphs from the Skues and Sawyer era; the early American nymphs (those from the mid-to-end of the twentieth century tied mainly with soft, natural materials such as feathers and animal fur dubbings); and then those of this current era, which tend to be constructed of hard, brightly colored materials.

Trout nymphing in North America is, in my estimation, the most effective, complex, and popular way to fly fish for trout. I'd like to recommend that *Trout* readers find a copy of *Masters on the Nymph*. It features an amazing lineup of now-historic and twentieth-century experts who accurately capture the full essence and scope of the nymph fly's creation, development, and popularity in our sport of fly fishing for trout.

Recommended: *Masters of the Nymph* by J. Michael and Leonard Wright Jr. 1979. Nick Lyons Books-Doubleday. Illustrated by Dave Whitlock.

Classic Feathered Trout Streamers

The streamer fly is a long-bodied design that imitates small forage fish that are prey for trout, char, and land-locked salmon. These streamers were developed to catch larger trout that feed on quantities of minnows, trout parr, and other small fish as the trout mature and require more food intake in order to continue growing.

There is evidence that streamer lures were used by non-flyfishermen in ancient Macedonia and by early Alaska Eskimos, but the design is first known in North America from the very late 1800s. It is recorded in our fly-fishing literature that around 1890 to 1901, Herbert L Welch, of Mooselook-meguntic, Maine, tied some of the first true streamer flies to imitate forage fish that occur in the northeastern waters of the United States. His flies—Welch Rarebit, Black Ghost, Jane Craig, Green Spot, and Welch Montreal—were apparently all very effective in the early 1900s and remain as classic, popular streamers today.

Welch was one of the first American flyfishermen to realize that the diets of larger trout, char, and land-locks contained significant amounts of small fishes. Another streamer tier from Maine, Carrie Stevens (1882–1970), gets my vote for fashioning the most perfectly tied feather streamers. Her streamers stand alone for their design perfection, material proportions, and colorations, as well as their classic effectiveness and lasting popularity. I've included some of her streamers in the illustration. Carrie's "Grey Ghost" is said to be the best-known streamer fly throughout the fly-fishing world.

A close second for creating especially high-quality and beautiful streamers was Lew Oatman (1902–1959). Lew's Brook Trout, Male Dace, and Silver Darter are illustrated here, and one look will convince even the most critical eye that his work is pure classical excellence!

I was pleasantly surprised to learn, during my streamer history search, that Theodore Gordon had also created early streamers, although not initially for trout. His designs were to lure in pike, bass, and perch. However, his Bumble-Puppy streamer was eventually proven to be an excellent brown and brook trout fly, especially in low visibility waters and at night. It continues to appear on the "favorite fly lists" of many writers, even today.

Feather-bodied streamers for trout are usually constructed on long-shank, Limerick- or Sproat-bend hooks in sizes 10 are 1/0. The hook point is located at about two-thirds the length of the body. Tandem hooks in the mid-body and at the very tail are sometimes tied into streamers that are to be trolled or used to hook fish that tend to strike at a streamer's tail. The body feathers, originally called wings, are usually best constructed from cock necks or saddle hackles that are thin-stemmed and have a moderate- to wide-width web to give the fly the ideal fish shape and movement in the water. For the streamers with darker backs, peacock or ostrich herl are most ideal, and the

flexibility of these feathers complements the desired body movement of these flies.

Around 1975, Dave Inks and Doug Swisher introduced the New Zealand "Matuka" method for creating the body of the streamer. I've always felt that this method is incredibly effective for streamer shape and water performance; plus, this technique helps prevent tangling back the feathers around the hook when cast. To imitate the coloration and markings of natural foods, badger, cree, furnace, chinchilla, and grizzly hackles are unsurpassed. When carefully dyed or overlaid with other hackle colors, remarkably beautiful minnow body imitations are possible. Marabou feathers, ostrich and peacock herls can be used to simulate the lower belly and further enhance realism and swimming movement. The hackle stem admirably depicts the lateral line that all small fishes have along their sides from head to tail. Because predators are particularly triggered to attack prey when eye contact is made, most streamers are adorned with a pair of vivid eyes on their heads. The gorgeous, spotted neck feathers of the jungle cock are the classic feathers for eyes, but being endangered, this once-wild gamebird is now pen raised, and the feathers are expensive. A number of realistic jungle-cock imitations, paints, and plastic eyes have become available and are widely accepted by today's streamer tiers and fishermen.

Most small fish that trout feed on, such as shiners, dace, chubs, shad, smelt, and trout parr, display light, reflective side scales, especially when they are actively feeding or injured. Highly reflective metallic and pearlescent Mylar strands, such as Flashabou and Crystal Flash, incorporated into the streamer fly, completes the illusion of the live minnow. These graceful, long, slender flies, with their intricate coloring and neatly proportioned feather bodies, captivate both trout and the fly-fishermen's eyes. I love the challenge of illustrating these little works of art with my paints and pencils as much as sculpting them at my tying desk.

In my lifetime, I've watched streamers become even more effective as weights such as split shot, lead wire, metal beads, dumbbell eyes, and tungsten cones have become legal and accepted by flyfishermen. Sinking tip and full-sinking lines can further enhance the ability to reach swifter and deeper trout waters. Unlike most aquatic invertebrate imitations that should be fished with very precise water action, streamers are effective when worked up, down, or across-stream as long as one is imitating the action of minnows that are fleeing, feeding, or swimming. Quick directional changes, erratic pauses, and twitches often trigger a trout's predator instincts to attack the streamer. Joe Brooks, a devoted trout-streamer expert, often said that streamers worked best in current when presented so the trout could see a side view and in still waters when swum directly by a trout's nose. I often hear streamer flyfishermen remark that working streamers in flowing and still waters is much more interesting than drifting insect imitations. I, myself, love them both.

A good assortment of productive, feather-bodied streamers should match the sizes of minnows that trout feed on; have the color, shape, and action of the naturals; and be impressionistic, rather than an exact imitation. Try to add some black, white, and fluorescent color patterns to your fly box for when water visibility is limited by murkiness or low-light conditions.

Classic feather-bodied streamers still have an important place in one's fly box. As with most flies, streamer designs are continually evolving as our knowledge, materials, and methods are expanding.

To further your feather-streamer knowledge and tying methods, I recommend:

Stream Fly Tying and Fishing by Joseph D. Bates Jr. Stackpole Books, 1966.

The Founding Flies by Mike Valle. Stackpole Books, 2013.

Guide to Aquatic Trout Food by Dave Whitlock. Lyons Press, 1992.

For more of Dave Whitlock's perspectives on fly types, please revert back to his "Artful Angler" columns in *Trout* magazine, 2014 to 2016, and/or look for his upcoming book.

Prints of Dave's art appearing in *Trout* magazine are available at www.davewhitlock.com.

More Tips on Choosing Flies: TU Tips

Fishing Dries

Many fly fishermen prefer to fish dry flies and nothing else. They get no excitement fishing a subsurface nymph or streamer, preferring only to see that splash or sip on the surface as a nice brown or rainbow takes their offering.

I'm not a member of that school. I pride myself on how much my nymph fishing has improved over the years. Still, when fish are sipping flies on the surface, my adrenalin does get pumping.

Rising trout do not, of course, automatically equal hooked fish. There's an art to it, a process, to get it right. Consider this. You are moving slowly upstream, casting to the occasional rising fish as you go. Up ahead, the water in a small pool gushes over some rocks and empties into the pool you are now in. The distance to the head of the pool isn't far—perhaps 60 feet. As you watch, you see a subtle splash just below the rocks. There it is again. And there, 2 feet below the first rise, there's a dimple on the water. You can't see what the fish is feeding on, though there are some blue-winged olives on the water, so you've got a good idea what to do. You tie on a size 16 BWO and slowly continue upstream, trying to get into casting range. The water is clear. Is your shadow on the water? Don't let it be. Try a different approach if it is. The same with your fly rod and cast. If the line or rod is throwing a shadow onto the water, you're going to spook the fish before you even get your fly onto the water.

As you move into position, take care not to shuffle your feet and kick up gravel. This looks like a decent fish, so he's probably been caught before and equates underwater gravelly noises to being caught. Once you're within casting range, stop and watch. Observe. Don't do anything. Are you in a rush? Take your time. What do you see? Are the rises occurring at regular intervals? How regular? Are they in the same place, or are they moving around? Realize that the sip or rise you see on the water is probably a good foot or more in front of where the fish is actually holding. He may on occasion float back and pick up an insect downstream of his holding position, but you can't consider that as part of his regular feeding pattern.

In place? Ready for the cast? Try to have your BWO alight onto the water at least four feet above the fish's holding position. Make some false casts, but not too many. The more the line is in the air, the more chance the fish may detect it, the more chance you may make a mistake. When you shoot the line upstream, take care not to line the fish. You place your line directly over him and he will be gone. Try to angle the cast so only the fly will float over the fish. You can do this either because you have a good position to do so, or because you have turned your wrist during your release and have put a curve into the line.

Once the fly is on the water, throw a quick upstream mend so you'll get a longer drag-free float. Assuming all goes well, the fly will float naturally over the fish, and, if the timing is right, he'll rise and you can set the hook. If he doesn't rise, try again. Take your time, however. See if he comes up again or if, perhaps, you have spooked him. Stay at it. In time, you'll either hook him, put him down, or conclude that you have the wrong fly on. If the latter, keep watching the water, try to determine again what the fish is eating. Maybe the size 16 is too big.

It's all about figuring it all out, putting together the pieces, playing this remarkable game of chess on the water. And that's what attracts so many of us to fly fishing. Figuring things out, thinking it through, adjusting the game plan. What could be better?

—Jay Cassell, Katonah, New York

Classic terrestrial water—a spring creek in a grassy field.

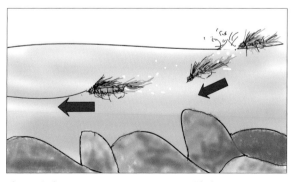

The atypical upstream streamer presentation with short strips can
be very effective.

Pat's Rubber Legs.

Tie Flies, Understand Real Bugs

Learn to tie. If you get set up to tie all your own flies, you *may* save some money, but you will certainly end up with 20 times the fly arsenal. The quantity of fly choices itself is not the reason your fishing will improve; it's the chances you will take and places you will be more likely to cast into knowing you can easily afford to lose some flies. You will no longer feel the need to wade out and spook a pool to retrieve a 3-nymph rig. You will snap it off and attempt to get your flies back after the pool is fished—maybe. Tying your own can give you an even better edge if you are willing to divert from the original, store-bought flies you started with and slowly convert them into custom-tweaked patterns perfectly engineered for the palates of your local trout.

—Jay Zimmerman, Boulder, Colorado

Follow a Path Less Traveled

The part of the world I fish most is full of small, clear, and very tight spring creeks. To most, that means delicate presentations of small dry flies, and sometimes I'll do just that. More and more, however, I'll tie on a leech pattern and fish it directly upstream using short, staccato jerks of my line (above) to make the leech behave like a wounded minnow; normally on a 2 or 3 weight. My friends chide me that my favorite leech pattern doesn't look much like a leech, that I certainly don't fish it like one, and that throwing streamers on a 2 weight is preposterous. But, the whole show works and it catches me a lot of fish.

The lesson is that following a path less (or perhaps not) traveled will sometimes get you lost. Other times, however, it will take you to great places, and sometimes those places are full of nice browns and brookies. Don't be afraid to try new things and techniques, or to go rogue perfecting strange arts that your friends will make fun of you about over a beer at the end of the day.

—Henry Koltz, Brookfield, Wisconsin

Rubber Legs Work

It seems like every time I wander through fly shops to check out the fly bins, more and more fly patterns are coming equipped with rubber legs. Even tried-and-true mayfly patterns, like the famous Green Drake pattern that makes early summer on British Columbia's Elk River perhaps the best dry-fly destination on earth, are sporting rubber legs. Rubber legs have been popular on high-floating terrestrials like hoppers and ants for years. But for the Royal Wulff? The venerable Adams? Yes, indeed.

And I've become a convert, frankly. Here's why: think of rubber legs as little outriggers that provide some stability for traditional flies—even parachute versions. These innocuous little strands of rubber jut out from the body of the fly just like outriggers on a Polynesian dugout. The result? A fly that floats upright and perfectly almost every single time, even in heavy water. And, judging by my own anecdotal research, the fish don't seem to mind. In fact, the vibrations of the flimsy little rubber legs might actually make flies more attractive to trout.

Try it and see if you agree. Next time you tie up a mess of Humpies or Stimulators, throw in a pair or rubber legs on either side of the fly. You'll be surprised at how well these traditional flies float, and I'm betting you won't notice a difference in your catch rate (unless it goes up, of course).

—Chris Hunt, Idaho Falls, Idaho

Don't Discount the Gear Guys

Fly fishers have a tendency to be insular, to mistakenly believe that fly fishing is a higher calling that far exceeds traditional gear angling in every sense. Perhaps that's why we're often perceived as a bit snooty and tweedy, and I think it's why the sport grows slowly when compared to traditional angling. I'll admit, to this day, I fight the urge to turn my nose up at the gear guys.

But, about 10 years ago, I went pike fishing in Saskatchewan for the first time. Prior to traveling to the north woods, I did some research on fly patterns and realized they were often very big, very gaudy, and very shiny. You know, kind of like those Krocodile and Dardevle lures that hardware guys throw

200 feet at a time and often reel in with a fish on the business end.

I did more research. Everybody told me wire leaders were vital. Gear guys, on the other hand, almost never used wire for toothy pike. Instead, they would use a bite leader—usually about a foot of 40-pound test line.

So, I got busy tying flies that looked like lures, and I showed up at Black Lake with a spool of 40-pound Maxima. The results? Stellar, of course. The lesson? Don't discount the gear guys—they know what they're doing (and not just for pike). Emulate. Borrow. Hell, steal intel. You'll be a better angler if you have an open mind.

—Chris Hunt

The Windshield Never Lies

The windshield never lies. I recently took a long drive through Kootenay, Banff, and Jasper national parks along the border with British Columbia and Alberta. Throughout the entire drive, delicious, glacial-tinted trout water paralleled my path. Trouble was, save for the lower Bow River in Alberta, most of that water isn't worth more than a cast or two. A lot of high-country rivers are the same way—the environment is so austere (rock and ice do not make great habitat for bugs and, therefore, for trout) that fishing isn't really an option.

But, when I finally arrived in the high-country resort town of Jasper, I knew I was back in trout country. Within miles of town, my windshield became a crime scene for green drakes and some smallish caddis. As I drove west out of town, I found myself spraying down the windshield every few minutes to wipe off the remnants of the hatch I just passed.

If you're not sure you're in trout country, check your windshield. If you never run out of wiper fluid, chances are you're not in a great place to fish.

—Chris Hunt

Hot Water

My new favorite fly-tying tip: to straighten out curved deceiver feathers and get them to tie in evenly, run them under hot water before tying. This one's straight from YouTube and not one I discovered on my own.

—Keith Curley

Mouse Flies

In late summer on a stream with hungry big browns and rainbows, try a mouse pattern. Sure, they look funny and maybe

you've thought of them as kind of a gag gift for anglers. But mouse patterns actually work.

Cast, keep the slack out of your line, and twitch the rod tip while retrieving in spastic little jerks to imitate a swimming mouse. This works great at dusk for browns. Hang on, they hit hard!

—Tom Reed

Don't Be Afraid

Don't be afraid to change your fly. If you've misread the hatch, and you need to offer something that more closely matches the fishes' food source, have at it. Sticking with a dud fly won't produce fun fishing. Also, pick your flies with the size of the river, your skills as a caster, and the amount of overgrowth in mind.

—Susie Leeson, Steamboat Springs, Colorado

Go Dark at Night

Fishing topwater at night? While it may seem illogical, use dark flies, not light ones. No matter how deep the sky, the fish are just seeing silhouettes, not colors, and a black fly will show better than a white.

—Mike Sepelak

Taming Mega-Hatches with Terrestrials

Everyone likes a mega-hatch, when flies come off in droves and just as many are stuck in the surface film tempting every trout in the stream. But, when mayfly and caddis hatches are dense, trout may be overly skeptical of your offerings, and they might, in fact, have trouble even finding your fly among the masses of real insects on the water. I've encountered that situation many times, especially on South-Central Idaho's Silver Creek, where clouds of Trico spinners fall to the water all at once, and the trout sucking them up turn that normally flat-surfaced spring creek into what appears to be a set of riffles. Expecting the creek's big rainbows and browns to find your size 22 Trico spinner among that mass of real flies can be maddening. When that type of situation occurs, be the angler who steps out of line and knot a terrestrial to the end of your tippet. These fish, even when keyed in on a particular hatch and sucking bugs down one after the other, often pounce on a terrestrial. And why wouldn't they—they would have to eat at least a hundred Trico spinners to equal the amount of protein they take in with just one grasshopper. Ants and beetles offer big results in a minimal amount of effort, too. Think about risk and reward, effort versus gain, and you'll quickly see why this tactic makes sense when you're fishing these mega-hatches, be it caddis, PMDs, Tricos, mahogany duns, or even Baetis.

—Greg Thomas, Missoula, Montana

Terrestrials (and a Goddard Caddis).

Go Different

You probably know this because it's hardly a secret, but don't get hung up on popular or traditional patterns. Sometimes, even on super-tough, technical water, fish will jump on something that's just different. I am thinking about a day on the Smith River tailwater here in Virginia one spring. When water is low, tailwater fish can be crazy technical. I was with

A nice brook trout landed on a dry fly.

a buddy who was fishing the stuff that can work: midges, tiny nymphs, and so on. He was struggling. So was I. So I switched flies and immediately hooked up. The fly? A Mickey Finn! My buddy was astounded. Later, I switched to this basic green nymph I'd been tying. Simple. Big. Ugly. Let's just say I outfished him. By a lot.

—Mark Taylor, Virgina

Brookies Like Red

Brookies like any fly with red on it.

—Scott Nugent

Go Opposite

Can't match the hatch—go completely opposite.

—Scott Nugent

When in Doubt

When in doubt, pull a stimulator out— ANY attractor pattern for that matter. Whether you use a Royal Wulff or a Trude, a good basic fly with a great profile can cover a lot of water and find any interested trout from below.

—Brian Kozminski, Boyne City, Michigan

Organize by Season

Organize your fly boxes by the time of year. Yes, BWOs and Adamses can go in any box, but rarely do I ever find the need to use a Hendrickson (light or dark) after I use a terrestrial. Early-season flies, middle-season flies, and late-season flies all should be separate; nymphs and streamers have their own Cliff Day Boxes I carry all year.

—Brian Kozminski

"Aha" Moment

My fly-fishing "Aha" moment was what I witnessed three mountain boys on the lower Cataloochee doing in the early 1970s. Prior to fishing, they collected stream samples, bugs, and flies from leaves, logs, and rocks. As one started imitating the samples on the vise, the other two geared up. They both took a few flies and went up the creek. A couple of hours later, they both had their creels full of 12- to 14-inch rainbow trout. A life-changing experience for me, and the best lesson I could have learned about fly fishing.

—Ron Gaddy, North Carolina,
Jonathan Creek School of Fly Fishing,
TU Cataloochee Chapter 427

The Rubber Band Caddis Nymph

One of my most effective flies is one I created. I call it the Rubber Band Caddis Nymph.

This is a very simple yet effective fly. The body is wrapped with a tan rubber band, creating a segmented look, a soft rubbery mouth feel for the fish, and a density that sinks well without added weight. The fly is finished with a couple wraps of black hackle.

—Richard W. Bender

When in Doubt, Choose Black

A suggestion for a tip on fly selection: when in doubt about color, in dim light, or in discolored water, choose black. It's most readily seen by trout under the latter conditions because of its opacity and is a common color of some trout food items in most watersheds.

—Basel H. "Bud" Brune, Virginia, Northern Shenandoah Valley Chapter, Virginia Council, TU

Give the Fish a Break

If a trout misses your dry fly or refuses it, move a short distance away. Give the fish a break; then go back with a different fly. That may be the one he is looking for.

—Dan Beistel, Oviedo, Florida

"A Little Black Nothing"

Use simple, effective flies that are generic imitations for insects on your local waters. An example is the soft hackle fly, especially with a black sparkle dubbing body and black hackle. It has been around for centuries, and it catches fish on lakes or streams.

In my state of Oregon, it may represent an alderfly, ant, beetle, caddis, or midge. Or many others. For your region, you may have to look for the likely hatches. Also, this fly is quick and easy to tie.

The first time I fished with my friend John, he asked for a suggestion of a fly to try. I showed him the black soft hackle. He exclaimed, "But that's just a little black nothing!" After using it for a few hours and catching 20 trout, he was very pleased with his new "killer fly."

—Erle Norman, Oregon, Tualatin Valley Chapter

Matching Soft-Hackle Wet Flies

Matching spring, summer, and fall hatches with soft-hackle wet flies (for example, the RS2 Variant Soft-Hackle Wet Fly) is easier than you may have assumed. For example:

- Sylvester Nemes's Peacock Herl fly: one of several over-looked flies for fishing for trout when they are taking midges on the surface. Although this particular soft-hackle is more of a hybrid variation and is **not** a true soft-hackle, its effectiveness at fooling finicky trout should not be overlooked.
- When nothing is hatching, my suggestion is that you prospect with a Hare's Ear soft-hackle and/or a Pheasant Tail soft-hackle as opposed to the standard nymph version of the same fly. The results may just surprise you.
- Want to make a Woolly Bugger twice as effective? Simply tie on a size 14 soft-hackle wet fly as a trailing fly off the bend of the hook of the larger Woolly Bugger and see which one the trout prefer. Once again, the results may surprise you.

—Michael Brucato

Size Down

Modern numbered dry-fly saddle hackle is great. If you are tying a size 12 mayfly dun, you know that the size 12 hackle will be correct. For most "down-wing" flies with palmered hackle, like Elk Hair Caddis and stimulators, though, go down one size in hackle. For instance, for a size 14 Elk Hair Caddis, use hackle labeled as size 16. The fly will float better and be less likely to tip over.

—Tom Wiensch

Seine the Water

My best tip to finding the right fly, especially if you are nymphing, is to seine the water before you start fishing. Spend $3.97 for a two-pack of five-gallon paint strainers at Home Depot, which will fit right over a net. Get a buddy to stir up the ground

and rocks a few feet upstream, while you stand downstream to catch all of the stirred-up bugs floating downstream. Or hold the net below, while you stir up the ground and rocks yourself. After 15 to 20 seconds, you should find an assortment of the aquatic life in the particular river. And, you never know what you'll find . . . leeches, big beautiful stoneflies, mayflies, fat green caddis pupa, huge crane larvae, white worms, tiny midges, etc. You'll quickly be able to key in on the type of bug, color, size, and life stage, which will significantly improve your probability of a successful day out on the water.

—Joe Newsum

See Your Fly
Fundamental. Because of my age and eyesight, I frequently fish with a big bright dry fly or a strike indicator and a dropper.

When the top fly passes through an eddy, swirl, or whirlpool, if it pauses or dips, set the hook. It is likely a fish. If not, you get another opportunity to practice and perfect your casting.

—Ronald Burke

Tying Your Fly

One of the most important things any fly tier can do is lay an even layer of thread on the hook. To accomplish this, attach the thread with a long, 3-to-4 inch long end approximately one eye length behind the eye of the hook. Next, hold the tag end up over the hook at a 45-degree angle while wrapping the thread base. By wrapping the thread over the tag end, you will find the thread slides down the tag end, resulting in a uniform layer of thread from the front to the back of the hook. Finally, trim the tag end and continue tying the fly.

—Martin R. Petersen, Naugatuck, Connecticut

Pink Terrestrials

I suppose those insects are always around in the warm months, and we anglers don't tend to fish terrestrial patterns that much in spring because the trout tend to focus on the hatches of mayflies, stoneflies, and caddis that are naturally occurring in abundance now. When there are olives on the water, for example, tossing a fuzzy hopper pattern into the mix usually doesn't work. In fact, that can shut down the rises in a hurry.

But there are windows when the hatches abate, and things go calm for a while. And during those times, I've found it to be far more effective to throw a terrestrial to tease a bite, rather than throwing the sporadic mayfly dry, hoping to simulate a hatch that really isn't happening.

Another thing I'm learning is that pink is the hot color in those situations. I have absolutely no idea why that is.

But give it a try and see if it works. During the lull, the terrestrial may just be the ticket. And when the hatch is on, tuck those big bugs back in the fly box.

—K. D.

Two Rules for Picking Flies

The good news was that I figured out the hot bug that (in part) won a Friends of the Upper Delaware River "One Bug" event. The bad news was that I wasn't the guy throwing it.

Instead, I broke my own cardinal rule, and I paid for it. Of course, hindsight is 20–20, but it's good to review your mental game film, whether good or bad, after you go fishing. Understanding your mistakes is what helps you improve, and I will definitely learn from this one.

My failure was that I didn't spend enough time looking at the water before I selected my fly. Instead, I went with an all-day strategy. I wanted to fish a big, durable fly, and I wanted a fly that I could easily spot on the water. I had heard all the reports, and word was that March Browns were starting to happen. So I chose a March Brown emerger dry fly and decided to hope for a hatch, rather than going with what was already apparent on the water. I was dumb. I ended up seeing about 8 March Brown naturals over the course of the next 8 hours.

Meanwhile, a steady flotilla of Blue-Winged Olives, and slightly fewer Hendricksons, littered the surface all day, and the trout ate them, albeit sporadically. The Hendos and Olives were there at the start, and they were there at the end. The answer was right in front of me.

Granted, had the March Browns shown up in force, I could have gone from zero to hero in about 20 minutes. But that didn't happen.

Here are my takeaways.

Rule 1. Watch the water before you pick a fly. I picked my fly in the parking lot.

Rule 2. Don't try to impose your will on the fish. Listen to what the fish are telling you. I wanted very much to fish a sturdy bug and heavy tippet. But the fish told me to fish a size 14 loop-winged emerged pattern on 5X. I just didn't listen.

—K. D.

Pay Attention

Where there are naturals, make it look natural, and where there aren't naturals, make them pay attention.

—Tim Romano, Boulder, Colorado

More on Choosing Your Fly Color

How important is color when selecting a fly pattern? My answer is usually mixed: I think fly color is really important when you are trying to match natural insects, and not as important (or, better said, still important but in a different way) when you are trying to earn a bite with an attractor pattern.

I remember talking about this specifically with the late, great Dr. Robert Behnke ("Dr. Trout"), who explained that fish see colors, but differently than the human eye does. Trout better perceive the blue side of the spectrum (especially in the underwater environment), which is why things like purple Prince Nymphs work really well, even though you can turn over a million river rocks and never find anything that even closely resembles a purple Prince Nymph. Use blues and purples and such on attractor flies (especially patterns for underwater) because they are literally eye-catchers.

Purple dry flies, on the other hand, seem like a gimmick to me. At least I've never had much success with them.

I get asked most about streamers. And the answer there is, I always have four colors in my fly box, no matter what: black, olive, orange (or brown), and white. Chartreuse, purple, and red are also key colors.

I do subscribe to the "dirty water, darker fly" rule of thumb, so that's when I lean on black patterns. Clear water, a little white streamer is good. Anywhere that crayfish are found, and in tannic water, that orange/rust/brown mix is great. Olive is the all-arounder.

And when you are plain old prospecting, and hoping, gaudy is great. I like them looking like a clown convention. But in that case, size and profile are also key factors.

Of course, where you throw it, how you move it, what depth you fish it, how fast you strip it, etc., are all important ingredients in the streamer mix. More important than color, I'd say. Adjust those things several times before you switch bugs. If your streamer isn't getting bit, odds are, it isn't the color of the bug that's the main problem.

—K. D.

A True Gem: The Mole Fly

Most of the Colorado guides I know reserve a few rows of their favorite dry-fly boxes for a simple little Charlie Craven pattern called the "Mole" fly. After fishing more dry-fly imitations than I can remember, the Mole stands out as the most deadly effective dry-fly pattern for when trout are highly selective and keyed on small mayflies, particularly *baetis*.

I love a size 18 parachute Adams, as I believe that, presented right, that bug will tackle 90 percent of dry-fly challenges. But when I have encountered that other 10 percent, it's the Mole fly that saves the day. I've seen it many times: show the fish 10 different dry flies, and finally solve the riddle with the Mole. I should probably lead with the Mole. But it's fun to watch its effectiveness with some context.

The pattern is proof that simpler is often better. This fly doesn't take many steps to tie. It's just thread, beaver fur dubbing, and a CDC wing. Craven is brilliant for keeping patterns streamlined and simple. Sometimes that little extra flash or that extra wrap of color does ten times more for the angler's eyes than it does for the fish. Overkill can put trout off. I think about 75 percent of dry flies and nymphs sold through fly shops these days are probably overkilled.

One last point: never underestimate the power of CDC. Cul-de-canard. The end of the duck (the feathers literally come from the duck's backside). Naturally buoyant, CDC makes the most realistic wings, especially on dry flies. But CDC gets gunked up and is hard to float after a fish or two has bit the fly. The key to fixing that is using a scant dab of Tiemco Dry Magic before the first cast, rubbing off excess with a Wonder Cloth or felt rag. The better you treat the CDC with gel (but be sure the feathers aren't matted), the longer the ride lasts.

—K. D.

Match Your Fly Rod to Fly Size, Not Fish

Jerry Siem is the chief rod designer for Sage. He is one of the best casters on the planet, and he's been pushing the design envelope for the world's largest fly rod manufacturer for years.

On a tour of the Sage factory a few years ago, my friend Louis Cahill of "Gink & Gasoline" asked Jerry a great question (and I paraphrase): "What attribute are you looking most to capture when you design a fly rod?" Jerry's answer: "I want you to be able to fish all day, and at the end, not feel as if you have been casting a rod at all."

According to Jerry, anglers often spend too much time trying to match the rods they use to the species they chase, when in fact, they should be matching rods to the flies they use. For example, you think, "I'm after rainbow trout so I'm going to use a 5 weight." We know that roughly half of the rods Sage sells in total are 9-foot size 5-weights because there are a lot of trout anglers who think that way. However, if you are going to throw foamy mouse patterns all day, don't do that with a 5-weight. Use a 6- or 7-weight. You'll beat yourself up less, and you will cast.

Oh, Sage will sell you all the different rods for different fish you want. Just don't spend too much time thinking about the fish, and too little thinking about the fly.

—K. D.

Different Posts for Different Light

Guide Pete Cardinal reminded me of this one as we fished the Missouri River in Montana in early fall. It's hard to beat a Parachute Adams as an all-round, do-anything dry fly. With a good cast, and a better drift, the Adams will fool most trout. I'll fish that pattern during almost any mayfly hatch, and the only real consideration is adjusting size to match the naturals. But there's one other consideration that can make a huge difference when the trout are subtly sipping.

Depending on where the sun is over the run, the water surface will either have a "flat" muted finish, or a "glossy" metallic sheen. If you are targeting fish in that flat gray water, use a Parachute Adams with the standard white calf tail (or synthetic) post. But if you're casting into the shiny glare, use a fly with a black post. Most of those calf tails for fly tying come in black and white. Use the whole tail, and tie equal numbers of black and white posts. (Non-tiers can buy black post patterns from many fly shops, including Dan Bailey's in Livingston, Montana).

Switching post colors will help you see your fly better, detect strikes better, and improve your hookup ratio by at least 50 percent.

—K. D.

The black post dry fly solves many glare issues.

CHAPTER 3

10 Things You Should Know about Reading Water

You've gotten yourself in the game by developing and honing a cast that can deliver a fly where you want it to land. You also have figured out which fly pattern to tie on in the first place. You either matched the hatch by observing what's

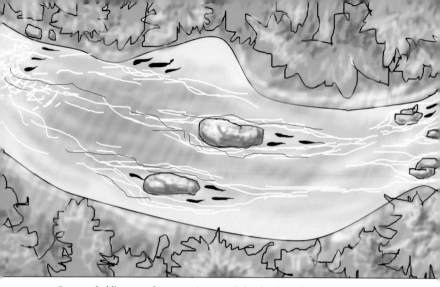

Common holding spots for trout—in seams, behind rocks, in front of rocks, and along the bank.

happening all around you, or you devised a plan to trick the fish you know are there with an attractor, in effect, making them an offer they cannot refuse. None of that matters if you cannot anticipate where the trout are going to be hiding and holding in the first place. "Reading water" is "high art" for the angler, and an extremely important aspect of the game. If you see the fish, great, you know where to cast. But it takes skill to find the fish in the first place, especially when they aren't revealing themselves by feeding off the water surface. Beyond that, knowing exactly where trout are going to be and why is a matter of instinct and anticipation. That definitely improves with experience. The more you fish, the more that gut instinct directs your casts. But there are some basic rules that will help you move beyond the guessing game, into a realm where you are actually dictating the action, and *that's* when fly fishing gets really interesting and enjoyable.

1. All Fish Love *Changes*

My close fishing buddies tease me about this now, because they've heard me say this so many times, over and over. But when it comes to targeting casts at ANY fish species with a fly rod, this is the golden rule. When I'm with an absolute beginner who is looking anxiously at the water and wondering where the heck they should cast the fly, this is always my first piece of advice. It's never failed.

Look for changes. Changes might be where fast current meets slow current, or shallow water transitions to deep water. Changes also include structure; where there is structure changing an otherwise uniform bank or river bottom. Color changes often indicate depth and structure changes. Those transition areas, where water goes from fast to slow, or shallow to deep, or unblocked to blocked… that's usually where the trout are going to hang.

As I approach a run, if I see two or three changes in the same spot, like a color change, a current seam (caused by structure) and maybe a dropoff, that's exactly where I'm going to pinpoint my first cast when I am prospecting for trout. The more changes the better.

Flat, even, uniform water is a total crap-shoot. Go ahead and try. It might work. But spend 90 percent of your effort focused on "change" water, and you will improve your efficiency by 90 percent.

2. Flat Water and Moving Water, All the Same

That "change" rule is even more important when you are fishing a lake or a pond. Even the smartest bluewater captains working the ocean are looking for changes. (A floating mat of sea grass, or a shelf, or a current transition, often indicated by a color change.) In a lake, you want to be keyed on those transitions and changes closest to shallow water, because that's where most of the trout food lives. Sure, lake trout often cruise the depths looking for food. But we're talking about fly fishing, and trout that eat flies are trout that eat small baitfish and insects. So what are the changes? Weed mats, which are bug factories, and havens for small baitfish. Same can be said for drop-offs and shelves. In other words, it's all the same! It might be a little

bit harder to notice with the naked eye on a still pond than it is on a moving brook, but those trout will be in the "change" spots. And that's exactly why any serious trout angler should devote at least a little time every year to fishing lakes and ponds. That "ups" your game, keying into those subtle changes, and it's way easier to transpose this knowledge from flat water to moving water, than it is to take it from a moving river to a calm lake. Fish lakes for trout, at least once in a while, if only to take yourself to school.

3. Your Target Is Very Likely Closer Than You Think

I polled a number of my guide friends, and asked them what their number-one beef with clients was. All of them answered the same way: They set "Bob" up in the run to go to work . . . head downstream to help "Sue" . . . and when they come back to check on Bob, he's standing right in the middle of the run, stomping on the fish. Trout like to hang close to the bank, and the trout that are in shallow water, instead of sulking in the depths, are the "player" fish you actually have the best chance to catch. So don't bull-rush your way into the middle of the run, and stand on fish. Survey the opportunities very carefully, and start inches or feet from the bank. Only after you've eliminated or exhausted the opportunities that are closest to you, should you tread further into the river to chase the next target. And that should be a system you adopt, even when you know in your heart that the "choice" water is further away. Cover what's closest, and then move on, or out, or whatever.

4. The Buffet Line . . . Follow the Bubbles

Bubble lines are trout magnets. Condensed and compact bubble lines are better than loose lines. Those seams indicate where natural food is being collected and concentrated. You'll even notice, the more you fish seems like this, that the trout will actually time their eating in concert with what the bubbles are doing. As the seam expands and dissipates, the eats are more sporadic. When the bubble line compacts and is better defined, the trout get more active and eat more consistently. Why? Because the natural food is more abundant and easier

Do you see the big brown trout rising in front of that rock?

to consume, more efficiently. Sometimes, I'll even hold off on a cast into a seam, and wait for the bubble line to pack, and then put my fly in the mix, knowing that doing so increases my odds of hooking into a more willing player. That may sound like splitting hairs, but it works.

5. Trout Surf in Front of Rocks

We're all trained to look for that big trout hiding behind the rock, which is great. We should look for trout hiding in the seams created by rocks and logs, and such. But, sometimes, the biggest trout like to ride the "pillow," a natural hydraulic cushion created when a river current rolls off and around the front of a rock. When I'm working downstream-up, I always make a few casts in front of that big rock that creates the run. And when I am streamer fishing, or swinging wet flies, that cushion spot in front of the boulder in the stream is target A. Don't ever neglect the front (upstream) edges of rocks as you are working a river, even a fast-rolling freestone stream. I've caught more fish that surprised me, not only in terms of their mere presence, but also in terms of their size and aggressiveness, in *front* of the rocks than I have working the more predictable seams behind the rocks.

6. Seeing Is Believing (Be a Sight Angler)

Sight fishing, be it for trout, bonefish, tarpon, or bass, is the top of the fly-fishing game. You see the target, you make the cast, the fish eats the fly. That's as good as it gets. That's "pure" fishing, because that's where the fishing game meets the hunting game. That's a completely honest, fair match of skill versus instinct. It's something every trout angler should endeavor to experience as often as possible.

So how do you become a better sight-angler? The key is knowing what to look for. As my friend Joe Demalderis, who guides the Upper Delaware, once told me, "You are looking for a single star in the night sky, not the whole sky." A glimmer. A trace. A subtle flash. Eliminate the things that are not fish, and hone in on the telltales that might indicate the real deal.

If you're looking for a whole fish when you are sight fishing for trout, more often than not, you are chasing a pipe dream. Sure, sometimes, they'll reveal themselves in full, and you'll know exactly what to do. But you want to train your mind to look for trout parts, rather than whole trout.

You also want to look for motions and movements. Rocks don't swim. Weeds swing and sway in the current, but they look completely different than a trout does.

The key is to work a process of elimination. Look at a specific piece of water, and eliminate all the things that are not trout. Then move on, and fix your gaze on the next piece of water. When you get suspicious, look harder, and get ready to cast. When you are convinced, make the cast. But don't waste casts on

suspicion. Scrutinize to the point where you really trust yourself. Of course, a great pair of polarized glasses that fit the light conditions (light lenses on cloudy days, mirrored lenses on bright days, and copper or amber as a solid all-around choice for most trout rivers) will help you more than the naked eye ever will.

7. Trout Find Shallow Water for a Reason

I've always wondered about the angler who will see a laid-up trout in skinny water, but will still toss a weighted-nymph

rig into the deeper heart of a run. That's their prerogative, of course, but the seasoned angler knows that the trout finning in skinny water is exposing itself to danger for a very specific reason. That fish is there to eat. It might be picking off dry flies. If you stay and watch long enough, it will show you exactly if that's what it's up to or not. Even if you don't see rings and rises, you can assume that trout is sipping emergers or picking off nymphs. I'd lock on that fish, and spend all my time trying to figure that puzzle out, before I write it off and go barging into a run.

8. Be the Fish

Ultimately, when it comes to reading a river, you have to ask yourself one very simple question: If I were a trout, where would

I be? That sounds silly, but when you factor in all the things we've been talking about here, and then match your human brain against an animal whose brain is roughly the size of an almond, odds are, you're going to be right! I've spent hours underwater in scuba gear, and have exhausted many air tanks watching trout in rivers. I've seen strange things I never expected to see. But the trout are almost always where I think they are going to  be. And the interesting thing is that they don't leave when I join them. I suspect that's because they've never seen a giant black-neoprene-clad bubble-blowing blob like me ever before, so they simply don't know how to process that. They just do their thing. Shadows from above, like birds, or fly lines, freak them out, and they split (so don't over-cast a run). But trout hang out where they want to hang out, and it takes more than you think to move them from their comfort zone. (Don't worry about the kayaker or the tuber who floats over the run; the trout completely reset and resume normal activity less than a minute after the shadow passes. Trust me, I've seen it happen).

9. Clear Water / Dirty Water

Another important aspect of reading is understanding what the water clarity factor is, and how trout behave differently in different conditions. Trout eat in dirty water, sometimes more often than they do in clear water. With an abundance of food washing down, those opportunist fish are going to grab a lot of what is floating by. In fact, from the scuba experiments, I've learned that trout almost always inhale much of what floats by them. They suck in leaves, and sticks, as well as leeches and bugs, and they immediately spit out or eject what they don't like. But they err on the side of eating, not rejecting. When you are nymph fishing, if you hit them in the face with your fly, they're probably going to eat it. Whether you can react fast enough to set the hook is a different story. That's what the strike indicator is for, and we can talk about the pros and cons there on a different day.

For now, remember that as you are reading water, if the river is stained or cloudy, you need to pinpoint your casts and flies in even closer proximity to where you think the fish will be. In dirty water, make three casts in a spot where you might otherwise only place one good cast, just to cover your bases. Move much, much slower, and more deliberately in dirty water than you would in clear water. And the old adage that dark flies work best in dark water is a truth you should trust.

10. Always Think about What Might Happen Next

Lastly, reading water and planning to fish a run is 90 percent about where you want to place that fly and earn a bite in the first place. But that last 10 percent should be reserved for thinking about "what if." What if the fish eats here? What do I expect its next move to be? In my mind it's unethical if you cast to and hook a trout in a thicket of brushy water, when you know in your heart that the likely outcome is that the fish will burrow down into the wood and break your tippet, maybe even resulting in being tied to a tree stump rather than your rod. I always know where my landing spot is going to be, before I make the cast that may or may not hook the fish. It's only fair that we consider an ethical and reasonable end game, before we start the fight in the first place.

More Tips on Reading Trout Water: TU Tips

Wood Is Good—Foam Is Home

There is no truer truism that I know. If you're thinking like a trout, you will catch trout. If you've retrained your brain to

When fishing a wide river like this one, you want to visualize the "minirivers" from bank to bank to guess where the trout might be.

approach a stream in pursuit of log piles and foam lines, you will catch large trout. Wood is good. Foam is home.

—Beverly Smith, Jackson, Wyoming

Breaking a River Down to Size

At some point, every angler will step into the water and be intimidated, if not perplexed, by the river facing them. This may be especially true on broad Western trout waters that stretch more than 50 yards wide. All of the water may look good, and you may choose to fish as much of it as you can reach—either by lengthy casts or wading into the water to cover a greater area—but the fish are unlikely to be spread evenly across the river. In fact, on most rivers, a majority of trout hold in a specific area between one bank and the other, often in a piece of water that's no more than a few feet wide and several yards long, constituting no more than a percent or two of the total surface area. Why? Because this sliver of water, unlike the other 99 percent of it, offers exactly what those fish need, meaning a place to rest, a place to casually feed, and a place that is deep enough to keep them concealed from predators. In most cases, this water is revealed by a slick surface located between faster currents on either side of it. This may occur five yards off shore or in the middle of the river, but wherever you find it, you will find trout. So take time when approaching a large river and look for these "slicks" before you start firing blind casts from the bank. Once found, finessing a drag-free drift with a dry fly or nymphs, which is what these fish typically demand, is up to you. My suggestion: wade as close to these slicks as possible before attempting a cast.

—Greg Thomas, Missoula, Montana

Sight Fish Smart: Watch and Learn

Upon seeing a trout, many anglers immediately begin to cast to the fish. Not me. I prefer to watch the fish before I attempt to approach or catch it. You can learn much through observation, and in many cases it can be the largest contributing factor to a successful hookup. I mentally take behavioral notes and let the fish tell me exactly how to make my next move. Here are a few of my thought processes as I watch a trout:

- Is the trout rising? If so, to adults or emergers? If not, can it be seen feeding subsurface?
- Does the trout move regularly, or does it stay in one specific holding area? Sometimes trout will move very predictably

throughout a pool, allowing you to lead your target well in advance.

- When the fish feeds, does it favor a certain direction? Sometimes, trout will favor their left or right side when taking prey items. River current, visibility of prey items, and exposure/vulnerability can all contribute to this.
- How aggressive is the fish? Is it competing against other trout for prey items or for a prime feeding lie? Is it feeding often or selectively?

These questions are just starting points, so make sure you watch and learn from the trout next time you are on the water. I trust you will find that your patience will pay off as you become a student of your quarry.

—Chris Johnson, Round Rock, Texas

I've never met a trout that didn't love a good cut bank.

Think Like a Fish

When you are out fishing and are on new water, trying to find fish, remember that fish are basically lazy, just like human beings. They don't really like to work any harder than they have to, and they want to feel safe. So think about where the softest current with the most food going by might be that appears the best protected, and cast in those areas if you hope to take the bigger fish. The smaller fish are going to be in the areas the big fish aren't kicking them out of, which also tend to be the areas easiest for a fisherman to reach and fish.

—Nanci Morris-Lyon, Bristol Bay, Alaska

Reading Water Vertically

Most anglers are taught how to read the water by observing what's happening on the surface—riffles, runs, eddies, seams. I believe they need to look beyond the surface and understand what's happening underneath, all the way to the bottom. Read the stream vertically as well as horizontally. Water velocity can vary widely from the surface to the stream bottom. A dead-drifted strike indicator on the surface is actually dragging a nymph along the bottom at a very unnatural speed. The friction of water against the stream bottom dramatically slows down the flow in this zone, so it can be difficult to get a natural drift with the surface current pulling your indicator and line along at a much faster rate. Whether it be additional weight on the fly, more persistent mending of the line, or specially constructed leaders that allow the fly to sink more easily, it's imperative the angler learn how to better control the drift of their fly when it's not visible.

—Jimmy Harris, Georgia

Walk on By

He keeps rising and I keep casting.

It's a big brown, eating something I can't see in an eddy on the far side of a deep, swift channel. I throw the biggest upstream mend I can, then another. I flick the fly into the back of the eddy and make repeated mends. I change flies, then shift tactics to big and ugly flies with the hope of drawing him out of his lair. I switch back, add tippet. Change flies again. I wade to the top of my waders and high stick my mend. I take on a little water—it's cold but not intolerable. I still can't move him. I move to shallow water and start rifling through my fly boxes for the tenth time, looking for an answer—only it's too dark to see. The day is gone. There are fish rising all over the river, some within casting distance.

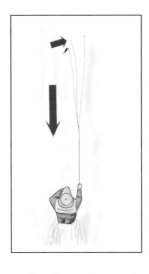

There are few things harder to walk away from than a rising fish, but sometimes you have to walk on by.

—Greg McReynolds,
Pocatello, Idaho

Fish Close First

Many anglers wade into the water as quickly as possible without realizing they could be spooking fish along the way . . . and it won't hurt until that big brown you thought was across the river darts from a boulder right next to your feet. So next time you're approaching a fishy-looking run, try casting first to the area through which you plan to walk . . . even if it doesn't look like it will hold fish. Who knows? A quick flip of the fly might produce an unlikely great fish. Having fished the near water first, you can move on to the prime run without missing an easy opportunity.

—Jim Hickey, Jackson, Wyoming

Trout will often look out toward the main current for food.

On Good Runs, Fish All the Water

Late-summer cutthroat trout are notorious for two things: a slow rise to a dry fly and feeding in the tightest of spots. I once watched a well-known fly-fishing television personality fish a fantastic run on the Grey's River in Wyoming. The main current met a point in a meander, forming a perfect eddy and eddy line. He fished it well, covering all of the water with expertise and landing one 15-inch Snake River, fine-spotted cutthroat. I watched the whole time and he never hit the very top of the run, the very point of the eddy where the water made an upside-down "V" with the bank on the left-hand side of the "V" and the eddy line on the right. It was about a 4-inch target. Finally, he gave up. I stepped up and made one cast into that spot, landing a big foamy hopper right next to the bank, and a big cutthroat came up slowly and took it. I landed and released a 19-inch fish.

The lesson? On good runs, fish all the water. Cutthroat in particular are right up against the bank in the smallest of seams and buckets. It's where they feel safe from predators and can usually be out of the sunlight.

—Tom Reed, Pony, Montana

Look and Listen for Fish

On native trout water in some parts of the West, sometimes large chunks of water seem unoccupied, making you think that maybe the stream is completely barren. Not so. Cutthroat love to occupy certain stretches of habitat and leave other stretches blank, particularly with fluvial fish that run up a small stream from another water like a river or lake. Get some good polarized sunglasses and learn to sneak along a stream, looking for fish. Listen for fish. I once discovered a big Yellowstone cutthroat in little water because I heard his rise behind a willow as I approached. I caught and released him. He was 20 inches and was up out of a lake downstream about 6 miles.

—Tom Reed

Patience and Deliberation Count for a Lot

Move slowly toward the river, and stalk patiently. It's very easy to spook fish away before you've even thrown your first cast by not being quiet and mindful.

Once you've stepped into the stream, don't rush. Work the whole stretch in front of you systematically before moving on. Patience and deliberation count for a lot.

—Susie Leeson, Steamboat Springs, Colorado

Juvenile trout will often cling to the safety of the shallows.

Fish the Edges

Fish the edges. The edges of banks. The edges of seams. The edges of deep to shallow. The edges of warm to cold. The edges of day to night. The edges of seasons. The edges of your life. It all happens at the edges.

—Mike Sepelak, North Carolina

The edge along the opposite bank is a prime holding spot for trout.

Go Fishing with the Local Fisheries Commission

Go fishing with the local fisheries commission. These guys are always on the water and usually will appreciate help. Walking up a stream with a net behind a guy with a backpack shocker will be humbling. It can be, ahem, shocking to see how many trout are in a run that you fish regularly and maybe catch one or two. Just as important, it will absolutely help you understand the kind of water where fish hold. Clear water. Maybe 18 inches deep. You don't see a fish. And boom! Up pops a 16-incher.

—Mark Taylor, Roanoke, Virgina

Have Someone Read to You

When I was learning to read books, I learned by having someone read to me. Soon I was able to pick out a word or two, then sentences, paragraphs, etc. Eventually, I was able read an entire book by myself.

Reading the water is similar. When I began trout fishing, almost all my fishing experiences were on lakes and ponds. Locating fish was a matter of looking for structure or depth. When I began trout fishing, I learned quickly that most of the time, I would be fishing moving water, which I had no experience with. My first five trips to my local trout river were fishless. Each piece of water looked as good as the next. Frustrated, I began asking questions and observing where others were fishing successfully . . . in other words, I asked those with more experience than I had to read (the water) to me.

Soon I could pick out one or two likely spots. Then a few more. Eventually, I was able to identify the most likely water on longer stretches by applying what worked in the smaller sections. Eventually, the entire stream became readable and less intimidating.

—Mark Dillow, Ex-Officio and
Texas State Council Chair

Fish All the Water

The best tip that I have gotten is to fish all the water, and that includes the water that you are about to step into on the way

to what you think is the prime water. Fish your way out there! Don't approach the bank too hastily or noisily. Make your first cast into the near water and work your way out.

—John Lin

Focus on the Experience

When I was a kid, fishing was all about catching the limit. A good day was a lot of fish in the creel, and a bad one was an empty basket.

Somewhere along the line, I realized that focusing on the day's take rather than the experience was a mistake. Once I did that, I started to catch more and bigger fish.

The change was simple: I just started making fewer casts and spending more time watching and enjoying the world I had intruded upon. Studying the water for a while and seeing a subtle rise or noticing a fin or a slight movement in the stream meant that one cast to the right spot usually sufficed. I didn't need to flail the water from one end of the pool to the other. Watching the insects leaving and entering the water and turning over a few rocks helped me to understand what was happening in the stream. This, in turn, gave me a much better chance of having the right fly on the end of the leader. And if I spent some quality time watching the birds and the sky and the scenery, I was much more relaxed and better at placing the fly exactly where it was needed.

This simple change in focus made me a better flyfisherman and certainly made each fishing trip more memorable.

—Greg Moore, Pueblo, Colorado

Watch for Beats

I wanted to share a tip that I have learned over the years fishing for native cutthroat trout in small, high-altitude lakes in the national and state parks, and wilderness areas of Colorado. These cutthroats cruise the shallows and mark out their own territories. I call them beats. If you are sight fishing to these fish, I find it best to slow down and watch them patrol their beat a few times before casting. They will typically follow the same pattern as they move around their area, and identifying this pattern will allow you to lay down your cast in the lane that you know they are going to return to momentarily. The best part of this technique is that it doesn't spook these wild fish because you don't have to lay your line over them. I'm sure this

As a bush plane swoops over-head, an Alaskan guide (with net) watches his angler (upstream, far right) slowly work his way from the near bank outward. Before you enter the water, make a point of fishing the edge closest to you first.

tip can convert to most trout species, but I've found it to be especially true when chasing cut-throats in Rocky Moun-tain National Park.

—Trevor Juth

Let Them Tell You

My number one tip is to think like a fish and to coordinate your efforts around what fish tell you, rather than imposing your will on them. I suppose that you could beat fish with nymphs all day and that eventually a trout will gag on a fly, or commit suicide because it doesn't want to deal with you anymore. But that doesn't make you a smart angler as much as it does a per-sistent one. (Granted, there are virtues to both.)

—K. D.

Cast Close

We all want to power out a cast upstream and three-quarters. But before you enter the stream, don't forget to cast to the water's edge nearest you. If the fish may hold on the water's edge across the river, they could just as likely be holding on the near side. Many times I have barreled into the river only to see a fleet of fish move away from my wake. Crouch to keep your profile low, and cast from the bank into the near water before physically entering the river.

—Chris Wood, Washington, D.C.

You Might Be Fishing Big Water, but You Should Still "Think Small"

Fishing big rivers can be intimidating. Large rivers contain complex patterns of habitat, some or all of which can contain fish. The best way to approach a bigger water body is to almost partition it in your mind into a series of smaller streams. For example, the riffle to the left has a nice hole under it. Fish the hole and move up to the riffle. The middle of the river has soft water on the edges of a run that looks inviting for trout. River right has a series of down trees in it where trout could be hiding. Think small on big rivers to catch a lot of fish.

—Chris Wood

Sight Fishing on Cloudy Days: Do These Things

1. **Wear yellow lenses.** Smith Optics has a lens called "Low Light Ignitor," which is a type of yellow, and it does noticeably improve visibility in tough conditions. I have no idea why that is, nor do I care. All I know is I see fish better with these lenses than I do with others on low-light days, and they have literally been the game saver many times.

2. **Slow your approach by at least 50 percent.** Your range of vision is, at least, half of what it would be on a bright day,

113

so you need to creep up on fish within 30 or 40 feet instead of 60 or 80 feet. You can't go bulldozing through the water. Little splashes and air bubbles will spook fish, so the only way to get in range is to wade quietly. The only way to wade quietly is to go slow. At least half speed.

3. **Look for signs of fish (or parts of fish), not the whole fish.** On a sunny day, you might see a shadow from 100 feet or more away. On a cloudy day, I shift my approach entirely and stop trying to look through the water, as much as I am studying the water itself. On cloudy days, I'm looking for wakes, pushes, nervous water, and that stuff. Of course, on a trout river, you want to look for rise forms.

4. **Take more "maybe" shots.** You don't have the luxury of being 100 percent certain in low-vis conditions, but if it looks like a target, go for it. Casts are for free. On a bright day, I'm all about casting economy and making every shot count, the first time. Wade into position, and set up for the perfect shot, factoring in the sun, shade, wind, and other variables. Under clouds, if you think you have a shot at what might be a fish, take it, and ask questions later.

5. **Let fish reset.** The good news about clouds and rain is that the fish have as hard a time (or harder time) seeing you just as you do them. So if you happen to be walking along and you bump a fish, watch it and see if it settles down. On a sunny day, that fish is likely to keep right on cruising, but in the clouds and rain, they'll often chill back out. Now that you know where they are, give them a cast and see what happens. Even a little flip cast at a fish that's moving away, but not panicked, can coax an eat now and then.

—K. D.

Sun and Shadows

More often than not, the sun and shadows will tell you where the trout will be hanging out. You'll inevitably become more adept at spotting fish when you learn where to begin looking. This doesn't apply everywhere, of course, but I tend to find 10 fish living and eating in shade pockets for each one I see exposed in a bright patch.

You don't want the trout staring into a bright glare, even if that means the shadows are not a factor. On the other hand, you should be sure to outcast your shadow when the sun is behind you, because a fish will still be spooked in flat light if it senses the motion of the line. When it comes down to it, analyze, but don't overanalyze—just know where the sun is, and where your shadows are. And know where the fish will feel more comfortable looking up, and take it from there. Just a little bit of understanding of the sun and shade will transform your fly-fishing game, probably more significantly than most anglers realize.

—K. D.

Fish Like Yogi

Yankee icon, 3 time American League MVP, 13-time World Series champion Yogi Berra will no doubt be remembered as

one of the greatest baseball players of all time. He'll also be remembered for his memorable quotes. Yogi said things that caused people to scratch their heads, perhaps even wonder how many times Number 8 took a foul ball off the chin. But the more one thinks about the quotes (which is what they caused you to do—a mental double take), the more they sink in for their, well, profundity:

"It's like déjà vu all over again."

"If you come to a fork in the road, take it."

"Nobody goes there anymore. It's too crowded."

I think about some of the fishing guides I know, and feel like Yogi would have been great at that job, too. Because the art of guiding is explaining things in ways that are beyond simple, so the lessons sink in right away. I've always remembered one Yogi-ism in particular when it comes to fishing. It's a lesson I cannot emphasize enough, and probably the best piece of advice (if not the most eloquent) an angler can ever hear: "You can observe a lot by watching."

In the fly-fishing context, what that means is that if you just take several minutes and watch the water, before you cast, so many of the other riddles of fly fishing—where to cast, how far, how deep, what fly to use, what color, what size, what drift, etc.—answer themselves. And it's sad how people will spend hours and hours perfecting a cast, or studying up on insects and hatches, only to render it all totally worthless by bulling through a run without watching what's going on first.

After all, Yogi also said: "Think? How the hell are you going to think and hit at the same time?" Substitute "cast" for "hit," and it makes perfect sense for the angler. The best anglers aren't running physics lessons through their minds when they see a brown trout rising 30 feet ahead of them—they're working off instinct. And that instinct works only if you've taken time to watch what's going on beforehand.

—K. D.

Microadjust

Don't fish the same track through the same run, every time you cast. Look for microcurrents, and microseams—small bubble lines, a color change, or a spot where fast and slow water meet, even within the same run that might be only five or six feet wide. Try to cover every line.

This was particularly clear to me when fishing for steelhead in Pulaski, New York. You could make the same drift through the same run 10 times, and then *bang,* you'd finally get hooked up. Is that a matter of beating the fish into submission? No, that almost never happens. More likely, that everything lined up in the microcurrent, the bug presented in the exact right place, moving at the right speed, and the fish ate.

Same thing happened fishing the North Fork of the Potomac River in Maryland. And that's almost always the case out West.

Microadjustments make all the difference. Sometimes that's a weight adjustment. Sometimes it's a matter of taking a closer, harder look at the water in the run you fish, and covering the microseams.

—K. D.

There's a 22-inch brown trout in this pool. Can you spot it?

CHAPTER 4

10 Things You Should Know about Fly Presentation

You've picked your fly. You read the river, and figured out exactly where to drop that fly. You made the cast to get the fly to the spot you chose . . .

Here's the kicker . . . You *might* be about halfway there. Because *presentation*—how your fly looks to trout in those few seconds after it hits the water—is about 50 percent of the entire game. Presentation (your drift) is as important, or more important, than all the things you did to choose the fly you want, figure out where to put it, then deliver it to the spot you chose in the first place. The most successful anglers are the most adept at presenting their flies. So here are some things you should know about this very important aspect of fly fishing.

1. You Will Never Beat a Trout into Submission

Okay, you may have whiffed on the first cast, so a second delivery of a dry fly (or emerger . . . or streamer) is sometimes warranted. But if you flog the water in the same spot, presumably at the same fish, with the same fly, over and over, your odds decrease—not increase—exponentially with every cast. That's almost counterintuitive for most of us who follow the old adage: "If at first you don't succeed, try, try again." But in fly fishing, it's better to remember that Einstein said: "The definition of insanity is doing the same thing over and over again and expecting different results."

If American anglers have an Achilles' heel, it's that we just cannot seem to process that information. "I've picked my bug, I'm doing everything right, and I'm going to make it happen, no matter what!"

But we can learn from our angling brethren from the South Island of New Zealand, for example, where the program goes more like this: You see a fish. You make a cast with a fly you think that fish will want to eat. Fly lands . . . you know the fish saw that fly. Fish doesn't eat that fly (sometimes that can be 15 feet away in the crystal-clear Kiwi waters). You stop. Right there. After one cast. And you switch fly patterns and wait several minutes. Then you show the fish plan B. No luck? Wait. Switch. Show 'em plan C. And so on and so forth until you a) either spook the fish off the run, or b) coax a take.

Understand that any trout, anywhere, is already wise to your first bug if it doesn't eat it, after the first well-placed cast.

Now, nymph fishing is a bit different because a trout wallowing low in the run is picking off food in many forms. It will inhale and either swallow, or quickly eject, pretty much anything that hits it in the face. Thus, the popularity of nymph fishing is that you can indeed force a bite, and hook that fish, provided you are quick enough on your reaction to the take. But in the "other," more popular forms (taking absolutely nothing away from nymph fishing, which is a unique challenge, in and of itself) where you're hoping to force a fish to actually make a decision to move and eat a fly—which is what dry-fly fishing and streamer fishing are—you need to check your ego at the door and be prepared to switch patterns. Follow the will of the trout, and don't try to impose your will on them. Learn how to do that, and you'll be operating on an entirely more effective, more honest, and more rewarding level of fly fishing.

The editor on a "Going Deep" story on trout for *Field & Stream* magazine.

2. Mending Can Be as Important as Casting

While the cast is obviously very important, you can lose the effectiveness of a great cast if you don't show the trout a good, clean drift once your fly hits the water. If your dry fly drags along the surface (or a nymph fly drags under the surface), trout will not be inclined to eat it, simply because it doesn't look anything at all like the natural bugs floating down the river, which the trout are keying on. Granted, there are situations when a skittering or skating dry fly looks *perfectly* natural, and a swimming or emerging nymph fly is *exactly* what the doctor ordered. But think about it . . . trout make a big portion of their living by eating hopeless, hapless insects floating in the current. So you want to replicate those bugs as efficiently as possible.

Mending—the art of lifting and placing your fly line in a way that allows for a perfect drag-free presentation—is the key to doing exactly that. In general, you want your fly line to be upstream of your leader and flies. Even if the current grabs and twirls your floating fly line, it won't create unnatural drag if that happens *upstream* of your bugs.

The mistake most anglers make when they mend is that they use a herky-jerky motion from waist level, and try to fling the line upstream of their flies. That might eventually get things set up

Don't stand in fast water when you can stand in calm. The current won't grab your line as much, and you will avoid microdrag.

where you want them to be, but that also wiggles the flies, and you lose valuable drift time by doing that.

Fly rods are long for a reason. They give you leverage. A great mend is accomplished by simply lifting and placing the fly line. Make the cast, let the fly float into range, then lift and place the line upstream to get a longer drift and presentation. Don't work too hard. It's an easy move, and if you do it perfectly, your line and leader will move, but your flies and/or strike indicator won't budge a bit.

But that takes practice. In fact, if you work half as hard at perfecting good mends as you practice your cast, your fishing efficiency will improve exponentially.

3. We Should Manage Foot Currents

Sometimes you don't really see the drag on your fly, but it's there, and the

Pay attention to the current at your feet. If it's moving faster than the current upstream, it can drag your line (and fly) without your even realizing it.

trout can notice it. Most often, that's caused by something most anglers never notice, because it's happening right at their feet.

You're casting upstream, and the current is bringing your line (and your flies) downstream naturally. And if you're doing things right, you're gathering the slack in your fly line, stripping it though your fingers, and letting it collect in the current at your feet.

But a problem can arise when the current at your feet (where the fly line is piling) is moving as fast or faster than the current you are casting into. That wash of current can grab the fly line and give it a tug, creating "microdrag," even if you're doing everything else correctly.

The fix is simple. Watch your feet before you cast. A step or two to the back, front, or side, to find some slack water to stand in, can make all the difference in the world.

4. Action (On the Fly) Can Be a Good Thing

You'll hear a lot of guides and experienced anglers talk about the importance of a "dead drift." (What I was just professing.) By that, they mean a fly must float on top of (or under) the water current in exact accordance with the flow—just as a natural insect trapped in the current would. Even a slight bit of drag or motion on a fly can make it appear unnatural, and trout will swim the other way, rather than chase it. Remember that as a rule of thumb, trout are lazy grazers, and they're going to key on the easiest-to-pick-off bugs, rather than go chasing the more difficult targets.

That said, sometimes you can make them an offer they can't refuse. Especially when you are fishing a big terrestrial fly, which looks like a T-bone steak to a trout. After the fly lands, a gentle twitch might just be the attention grabber you want. Same can be said for skating a caddis fly. Caddis flitter about and lay eggs on the water; they're in constant motion. It's okay to skate a caddis pattern. A dead-drifted caddis can be effective many times, but it might *not* be when the natural bugs are skittering about.

Same is true with emerging nymphs. How many times have you caught fish at the end of your drift, as the water naturally lifts your flies toward the surface? That's not a coincidence . . . that's what the natural bugs are doing down there, and you are looking the part.

The point is that you need to match not just the hatch, or the insect of choice. You need to match their behavior in terms of how you present that fly. Less is usually more, in that a gentle twitch or a nudge is good enough. You don't want the fly

looking like the Miss Budweiser racing boat ripping across the water. Just don't lock in on the notion that the only good drift is a dead drift, every time. Keep an open mind.

5. Tippet Size, Fluorocarbon, Monofilament . . . They Matter *Sometimes*

There is almost no trout you will catch on 7X (smaller) tippet with a cruddy drift that you cannot catch (and land easier) on 4X (larger) tippet, with a great drift. That's my opinion, and I'm entitled to it. I know there are many readers who might disagree with that. I know there are tippet manufacturers who definitely want you to believe you need seven different sizes of tippet on your person at all times when you are fishing. Take that for what it's really worth.

I have certainly fished on extremely technical spring creeks, with gin-clear water, where tippet size did indeed seem to be a factor. And I fished small tippet. I've also been on gin-clear spring creeks in New Zealand casting at very smart, old, 10-pound brown trout. There, knowing that we didn't have the option of landing a fish like that on cobweb-thin tippet, we fished an 8-pound test and still caught fish. It's all about the presentation.

Fluorocarbon sinks. Monofilament floats. Fluoro is stiffer with less stretch but is more invisible. Mono has more stretch. Fluoro is twice as expensive as mono, and that's the factor that really matters most to me.

6. Strike Indicators Are Bobbers

Let's just call them what they really are. I love fishing nymph patterns, and think that the strike indicator is key to effective high-stick, dead-drift nymphing. Having done a lot of scuba diving in rivers with trout and watching them feed, I can assure you that if you hit a trout directly in the face with a fly, it's going to eat it. The only question is whether or not you will react in time to hook the fish. About 50 percent hookups on grabs by trout is an incredibly good ratio, for even the most experienced angler.

If you fish with a strike indicator, plastic or cork bobbers are great for their durability and sensitivity. But yarn or wool—particularly white yarn or wool—blends in perfectly, in terms of shape and color, with the bubbles and foam on the surface of a river. And they make less noise when they hit the water. Factor in the type of water you are fishing (speed, waves, etc.) before picking an indicator. After that, the choice is entirely up to you.

7. There Should Be Reasons for Pairing Flies

It's hard not to like tandem rigs—two flies working together for the single purpose of making you happy. But there should always be rationale for the pairing. Sometimes that's merely to help you see better. I can't always see a size 20 Blue Winged

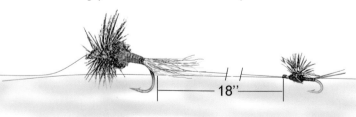

18"

The nymph on a dry-dropper rig should actually suspend anywhere between 1 to 2 feet beneath the dry fly.

Olive, so I put a highly visible size 14 H&L Variant just above it. If I see a rise or a splash near the H&L, I assume the BWO got bit, and set the hook. The tandem can also cover two stages of an insect. For example, the adult dry fly can lead the emerger and serve as strike indicator in the process. Hard to beat a size 16 Parachute Adams with a size 18 Barr Emerger or RS2 below it. The important point is to have rationale for every tandem rig you present. Variety for the sake of variety is not always a good thing. If you think you're covering your bases by matching two flies that don't reasonably work together . . . well, you are not.

A trout bursts from its hold behind a rock to grab the trailing fly on a dropper rig.

8. Trout Do Not Like Being Attacked by Food

This sounds absolutely silly, but that's exactly what it looks like—to a fat old brown trout—when you swim a streamer fly that is supposed to look like a baitfish, directly toward its mouth . . . or skitter a dry fly (because you missed the casting target by six inches) to the spot that just happens to be exactly overhead of a sipping cutthroat. Permit aren't used to crabs jumping toward their mouths, for that matter, and you'll even freak a shark out by dragging a big fly on a collision course with its toothy maw.

We anglers aspire to be perfect. We see fish. We cast the fly. We want the fly to be as close to fish as possible, because the closer it is, the more likely that the fish will see it. Fish sees fly, and fish eats fly. Right? Wrong.

A fly imitates a natural food source. Real minnows know they are food. They swim away from Mr. Brown Trout when they see him. Mayfly duns on the river surface are stuck in the current. The instant they don't look helpless is the instant they no longer look like food.

Sure, a trout's brain is the size of a marble, but you are ultimately tricking thousands of years of instinct. And one of the base instincts of a trout is to ignore those things that act really weird.

Thus, always consider your angles. Yes, you can dead drift a streamer like a Muddler Minnow, but that makes it look like a drowned grasshopper. If you want it to look like a sculpin, it has to swim. Put it just close enough for the trout to see it, and then make it look like it wants to escape.

9. You Want to Hit the Tail Light

In New Zealand, where the waters are typically very clear, and the trout are always very smart, the exact spot where a fly lands near a trout can matter down to the inch. The Kiwis will tell you that as you are casting upstream at a fish, it's always best to miss to the current side of the fish's position, rather than the slack, or bank, side. Sometimes you intentionally want to stick the fly off to that side. Indeed, there is nothing quite like watching a 10-pound brown trout take notice of a fly floating 12 feet away and off to the side, swim over, and grab it. The chances of that happening are often better than they are when the fly lands right overhead, or even if merely the tippet is directly overhead.

Guide Nic Robertson explained it to me like looking at the back of a truck. The trout is swimming several feet behind the truck, centered as if behind the license plate. The shore is to the left side. The main current is to the right. Your target is the right side tail light.

10. Your "Pace of Play" Matters

If you are working from upstream to down, say, swinging streamers for steelhead or salmon, it's important to cast, sweep, take a few steps, and cast again. In some places, like the Ridge Pool on the River Moy in County Mayo, Ireland, that's a courtesy shared by anglers. You rotate through the beat, and if nobody is moving, you can't get to the bottom of this classic run, where, whether you land a fish or not, you are rewarded, because you get to take a break and drink a pint of Guinness at Dougherty's Ridge Pool Bar.

There's also a functional reason to keep things moving, though. Too slow, and the fish is going to sense you coming. It will see just enough of the fly to be spooked. Conversely, if you go too fast, you'll skip right past the fish entirely.

Same is true when dry-fly fishing. If a trout senses that fly "climbing up its back," so to speak (because you are only moving a few inches at a time, casting inch by inch upstream as you go), you're going to spook it.

When you're matching naturals, of course, you want to put the fly where the fish are, and where the bugs are. Watch the rises and stick it right out front. But when you are prospecting and blind casting, you're better to keep moving. Too slow a pace, and you are your own worst enemy. You want that fly to simply, somehow, just *appear* to the trout. When it simply *appears*, they grab it.

Debate: Do Fly Line Colors Matter?

Some people think it's best to have a fly line you can see, so a yellow or orange line is a great thing. You can better watch your loops form as you cast, and then mend the line effectively as you fish. Great.

Others say that trout will sense a bright line, even as it is being cast overhead. Remember, the cone of vision for a trout extends up . . . out . . . and even a bit behind them, since their eyes are not only forward-facing, like human eyes.

So what's it going to be, better line control or stealth? The best answer is probably both. Go with as dull or natural a colored line that you can see, because trout *do* see fly lines, and they do spook on bright ones. But they also spook on bad casts and bad drifts.

More Things You Should Know about Fly Presentation

Give Terrestrials Some *Life*

Fishing terrestrials in late summer can be very productive . . . and there's nothing quite like fishing big bugs along grassy banks. In most trout-fishing situations, a drag-free drift is crucial, but not when it comes to fishing grasshopper patterns. Sometimes you have to give a little life to your fly. Just the other day, I was guiding some anglers who were dead-drifting hoppers with no success. I suggested they start "skitching" the fly—giving the fly a twitch or two and then letting it ride for 10 feet—and the fish turned onto the movement instantly. You shouldn't pop it like a bass bug, just skitch the hopper and let it ride. Too much movement can spook fish, but just enough can make them go berserk. Skitch it, let it ride . . . and get ready for savage strikes.

—Tim Linehan, Troy, Montana

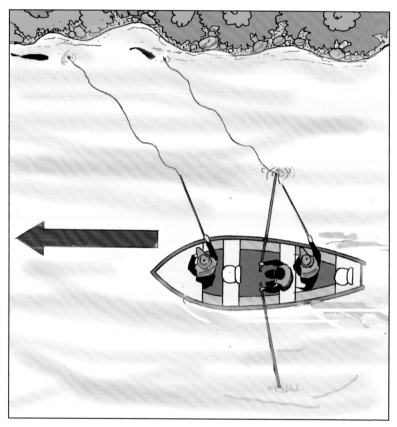

Drift boat etiquette: The angler in the bow should usually cast well downstream of the boat. The tail gunner's flies should land about even with the bow.

Enhance Your Profile

The transition that wading anglers make to being successful when drift boat fishing can be one of the great presentation challenges we all face. As a guide, I coach my clients to think not only about rod position, but also how the fly "looks" after the cast—how your imitation sits on or in the water.

Dry-fly anglers learn to cast downstream and across, resulting in a larger profile of the fly on the water. Down and across also works when swinging streamer or wet-fly patterns—fish see more of the fly when it's presented at the same angle as the line. Think of an imaginary line extending through the fly and keep it aligned with the rod tip and line. Mending keeps your line and fly "in the zone" longer, but a precise cast and well-presented fly increases takes—on big Western rivers like the Yakima in Washington, wild fish are smart and don't give anglers much room for error.

By presenting the fly with a wider profile, it gives the fish an opportunity to see it better and also improves hook sets—fewer misses equal more smiles from anglers!

—Derek Young, Ellensburg, Washington

Make Your Streamer Dance to the Beat of the Current

As anglers become more experienced, they want to catch bigger fish, and this inevitably leads them to streamer fishing. Presenting big, heavy flies to the largest fish in the river brings with it a whole new set of challenges, including a new way of thinking about presentation. Your presentation is no longer passive, but active, and it is the action of your fly that must excite the predatory instincts of the fish. With time you will find your own style of retrieve, and while it's fair to say that there is no "wrong way" to fish a streamer, there are some guidelines that will help you be more successful. One is the relationship between the speed of the water and the speed of your retrieve.

TROUT TIPS

Have you ever made an impulsive purchase that you later regretted? Then you have some insight into the mind of the fish who eats a streamer. Like a bargain shopper, fish don't like to miss an opportunity. Your fly must be a limited-time offer. If the fish has too much time to inspect and think his decision through, he'll decide to pass. On the other hand, no fish wants to engage in the pointless pursuit of a bullet train. Remember to think about the environment where the fish and fly meet. If the water is moving slowly, your fly should scorch off the bank, sending the message that it's now or never. If your fly is in fast-moving water, it's already moving quickly in relation to a holding trout. Slow your retrieve down and give the fly a twitching action like a wounded baitfish. Always remember, a predator takes what he wants. It's your job to make him want the fly.

—Louis Cahill, Atlanta, Georgia

Use Flies You Can Track *Under* the Water

Try using a Green Weenie as a lead fly when nymphing in streams that are small/shallow enough to be able to see your fly. It helps you to watch where your fly is drifting better than you can with an indicator (it can be surprising), and sometimes a trout will eat it. I only use that method occasionally, but the first several times I did it, I learned a lot about how variable your drifts can be depending on which way the current pushes your fly.

—Keith Curley

Go "Off Label" to Mix Presentations

A sink-tip line and a buoyant streamer (e.g., unweighted bow river bugger with a big deer hair head) can be a great way to fish streamers–gives a nice diving action to the fly and lets it stay up off the bottom while still being in the strike zone.

—Keith Curley

This big bow fell for an unweighted streamer fished on a sink-tip line. Note how the angler is carefully releasing the fish: with the fish pointing upstream, the angler gently cradles it, allowing it to regain its strength before swimming away.

Think *Inside* the Box

The area of awareness a trout is most likely to take the dry fly is an area approximately 3 inches in front of its nose and 2 inches to the side of either eye; I refer to this location as the "3x2 Box." A well-placed fly in this zone will, many times, produce a strike from a rising trout. The mistake many fly anglers make when casting to rising trout is casting too far upstream, an error creating two problems:

First, the drag (microdrag) of the leader or fly line (no matter how well you can mend) pulls the fly out of the trout's feeding zone (or, as I choose to describe it, the "area of awareness"); second, casting too far upstream to a rising trout gives the fish a better look at the fly, often resulting in a refusal.

Here is why I like the 3x2 Box: The angler, in not casting too far upstream, does not need to mend the fly line; instead, he/she is able to make short casts to either side of the trout's head, allowing for a quick drift past the fish and then recasting, drifting the fly past the trout's "area of awareness." Try it. It works.

—Conway Bowman,
Encinitas, California

The Smart Bomb: Tight-Line Nymphing in Fast Water

The challenges of fishing subsurface in high-gradient, boulder-strewn rivers during winter months can frustrate anglers of any skill level. Boulders in these streams create spaces between rocks where trout can spend much of their time feeding without emerging into the light of day. To make matters worse, heavy flows through these substrates can create complex currents that make strike detection difficult if not impossible. Solving this problem is easier than it seems; just use enough weight to keep your flies deep in the strike zone. Equipped with an adequately weighted rig, the angler's job is to maintain the tension by casting short, high sticking, and keeping the line as straight as possible through the drift. At times, you should actually drag your flies through a promising slot, not too fast, but just enough to keep things tight. Remember, fish in fast water don't have a lot of decision time and, therefore, must often strike on impulse. You should be able to feel most strikes on the tight line when you're fishing this way, so indicators aren't necessary. In this situation, they usually only distract the angler from what they should be doing: maintaining tension on the line.

—Toner Mitchell, Sante Fe, New Mexico

Sealing the Deal: The Pause Can Be Key on Dry-Fly Takes

You should wait a "Mississippi" before striking on a rising cutthroat. Fish goes up, opens his mouth, "One Mississippi," and then you lift your rod tip into him. Pulling away a dry from a rising cutthroat is the most common mistake on the water. See the white mouth? Wait until it disappears, then strike. Brown, rainbow, and brook trout all hit more quickly; cutthroats are unique in this aspect.

—Tom Reed

Small Water: Let 'Er Dance

On small streams, don't forget the value of the "skate" when dry-fly fishing. Standing upstream, let the fly dance and dap in the current downstream, keeping a nice tight line and avoiding creating a small wake with the fly. Just lift the fly and present it upstream again. Small stream trout can go wild for this technique.

—Tom Reed, Pony, Montana

You Have to Be Thinking about the *Whole* Enchilada

So here's my take on what goes through my peanut when I see a fish rising, or in a spot where I believe there is a great fish that I really want to catch. First, you have to concede that he's the king. He has every advantage and that's where I start, but at the same time, I convince myself I have a chance, too. I usually expect that I might have 1 or 2 shots at best (at that moment in time) to get him to come to my fly, so I slow down, way down, and prepare. I give the fish the ultimate respect he deserves and then try to do everything I can to even the odds. I sneak into the best position I can to make the best possible presentation. If he's rising, I wait to see what he is hungry for, is he eating all bugs or has he refined the menu? I tie on the "right bug" and believe in it. I check knots, grease fly, straighten leader. I watch his rhythm so I can time my cast to HIS schedule. I look upstream for any debris that might be floating his way, knowing I have to avoid it. I look at the bugs in his lane and plan to cast just in front of or behind a natural, depending on how the fish was feeding minutes before. I remember which way he was facing after he last ate: left, right, dropped back, moved up. I adjust my hat and clean my glasses, make sure my line won't catch on anything on my chest pack. I have my net

Dan Plummer instructing at the Bristol Bay Academy in Alaska.

close and look at how I will land the fish once hooked. I get my camera ready, take a deep breath and see it all happen in my mind, and then, last but not least, I look to where I last saw

my fish and wink at him. He knows that I have done all this for him, so I cut off my bug, turn for the bank, and relax. Poor guy never had a chance, I was perfect. I am "Troutboy."

—Dan Plummer, East Branch, New York

The Taper Is the Key to Presentation

Tapered dropper: When you use big, wind-resistant foam dries (standard Western style) and long, lighter tippet droppers, about 80 percent of the fishing day is spent untangling the dropper tippet from around the foam. You could heavy up the dropper tippet, but the dropper nymph won't sink fast enough, or the second dry might be overlined and not produce.

My brother and I devised the tapered dropper to minimize tangles and keep clients in the water. Simply tie a short stick of the same diameter tippet as the primary dry is tied on (in Missoula, that's typically 2X to 3X, even 1X during salmon fly hatch!). Four inches or less is plenty. Then tie the desired tippet size and length for the dropper with a triple surgeon or blood knot.

Not only will you spend less time tangled, you'll spend less time tying on after a break off. The dropper will break at the taper knot losing one fly instead of two. And in the end, the only constant in fly fishing is bug in the water always outfishes one in the hand.

—John Herzer, Missoula, Montana

Fly First Class

When you encounter picky trout feeding in large flat pools, consider the following dry-fly tactic I teach my clientele to fool the wild trout of the Upper Delaware River.

There are many variables within your control when stalking a trout on the dry fly. Of all the variables such as angler position, fly selection, and leader and tippet choice, none is more important than fly presentation. An accurate, clean drift is the key to consistently catching spooky trout on flat pools. The basics of the game stay the same if the angler is fishing from a boat or wading on foot.

When possible, the angler should approach feeding fish quietly and try to position himself upstream and across, optimally at a 30- to 45-degree angle above the trout. Try to keep your distance when fishing flat pools during low, water conditions. A 50- or 60-foot cast is not unusual in challenging conditions. The faster the water, the closer one can and should encroach. Once in position, wait to mark the exact position of the rising trout before you cast. This is the point where the downstream reach cast becomes an essential. I preach the importance of a long leader, accurate, and fly-first presentation whenever possible to my clientele. Try to use the longest leader you can cast reliably (my leaders are typically 14 to 16 feet from fly line to fly). The speed and characteristics of the current will dictate how far you need to place the fly above the rise. In most situations, 3 to 10 feet work for me. Pay attention to cross currents and try to make the first cast as accurate as possible. If the cast is not perfect, resist the temptation and don't fish it. Do not let the fish see the fly. Pull it back quickly but quietly, and recast. Try to reach cast far enough above the riser so that it minimizes the disturbance on the water but still provides a drag free float over the fish. If you have overcasted slightly, quickly and quietly move the fly so that it will line up with the fish downstream. Make sure that your leader and tippet are laid

Shadows spook trout. The lower you are, the closer you can get.

out behind the fly. Stack mend to keep the fly drifting drag-free. Remember that the fly should be the first thing the fish sees over its head. I believe that your odds of getting the take increase exponentially if you show the trout a fly-first, down-stream presentation on your first cast. If the trout stops rising, stop and wait until he reappears and gets back into a rhythm before you recast. I rarely have to go below 5X or 6X even in the toughest conditions with a downstream, fly-first approach.

—Darren Rist, Hancock, New York

The Angler Is Part of the "Presentation" Picture!

Remember that YOU are part of the overall "presentation" scenario. Thus, you should a) always (or at least usually) start fishing at the back of a pool of rising fish and b) dress to cam-ouflage yourself and match your background.

—Scott Nugent

144

It's Not a Railroad Crossing, But . . .

Upon arrival at the pond, jetty, or stream: stop, listen, and observe for at least five minutes. Check your gear and camera. Start catching. Have a nice day.

—Frank Steplar, Pioneer Chapter 276

You Learn How to Present Flies When You Have *Many* Targets

Two related bits of advice that, to me, are the most important to pass along to a would-be trout angler:

1. Go where the fish are.
2. Put yourself in the midst of them.

Despite fly fishing every stream in eastern Connecticut for a few years, and beating the Battenkill to death for two long weekends each year, it wasn't until I tried the Housatonic River that I discovered this for myself. The Housatonic was almost a two-hour ride from home, but in the 1980s it had just become a preeminent catch-and-release area.

I stood in the Sand Hole in late April, surrounded by 50 rising trout, in a position to try 1 fish until I spooked it or missed it, and then try another without even moving. Not a situation I had previously experienced! Or I could alternate casting to 5 or 6 trout, a method that generally prevented spooking them by repeatedly bumbled casts. I had a chance to try each Hendrickson imitation in my box and discover its effectiveness, or lack of it. The anglers surrounding me taught me by example. A few afternoons of this made for a better education than most of the preceding years.

Unless you are lucky enough to have a home river like this, you need to travel to find a lot of trout. Just as simple as it sounds, this does mean your organizational skills, research endeavors, and energy play as important a role as anything else during those initial times on the water.

—George Jacobi, Mansfield, Connecticut

Trust the Fly

Whether I'm fishing for striped bass in Massachusetts or trout in New Hampshire, my habit has been to choose a reliable fly pattern and stick with it. When not catching fish, I focus on presentation first and the fly last. On Alaska's Kenai River, a guide articulated this same philosophy almost as dogma: only after lengthening or shortening the leader, adding or subtracting split shot, or moving a strike indicator does he ever change the fly. The pattern may matter, he said, but presentation always matters more.

—Dave Cohen, Gloucester, Massachusetts

Up or Down? You Decide

Walk up on your fishing spot quietly. Do nothing for a while but watch what the fish are doing. Are they rising, nymphing, or frightened on the bottom? This gives a clue of what to do first when on the water.

—Carl Wachter

Give It a Lift . . .

When nymphing in a stream: at the end of the drift, pick up your rod tip to raise the fly toward the surface, then drop it down to let the fly settle. A following fish will strike at it as if it's eating an emerging nymph.

—Tom Morehouse, Orinda, California

Try an Alternative Nymph Prospecting Technique

This technique works best utilizing wet fly line, a 9-foot, 5X tapered leader, and a 5-foot, 5X tippet. It has been most successful in still water. Cast in a usual manner. Then let the nymph sink approximately 6 to 12 inches. Twitch the line approximately 6 inches toward you with your wrist. Let the line sink farther, and repeat until line has reached bottom. Then fish nymph as usual. The action of the nymph as it sinks

often triggers a strike, whereas the simple drop to the bottom does not.

—Ron Makovitch

Patience Is *Indeed* a Virtue

That was one of my mother's favorite sayings, and she would say it out loud as one of us would be testing hers. While it may be a virtue, it is also an effective tactic to be employed when trout fishing.

Here is a situation: You are looking at a seam that would be a good place to find a trout. Perhaps it curves into a back eddy where the debris of the river is collecting and swirling quietly upstream and around. You put your fly on a path to fish the seam, and when it enters the slower area you pull it out and recast.

Why not let your fly just sit there for a while? What's the rush? Do what is necessary with your leader (including making it longer or lifting it off the water) to prevent drag and just watch it. Even after it sinks, which it eventually will, give it a little more time. I think you will be surprised at the outcome.

Here is a case in point from a day on the Little Juniata:

Last year I fished it from the other side. I decided to not go across and settled in above the two large back eddies, watching the water for a while. I dapped a sulphur emerger in the NY tie—that is more yellow than the orange of the local version. A nice 12-incher took it. I moved farther down to cast in the swirling eddy of foam and miniwhirlpools. The drop-off is quick, so I was perched on the rock edge and cast carefully so as not to topple in. I switched to a sulphur parachute in a 14 and again a yellow body. Jim decided to switch from his 10-foot nymph rig to a dry-fly rod and went to the car.

As soon as he left, a good 15-inch fish took my fly out of the bubbles. When he returned, I gave him the particulars—long leader (12 foot), 6X tippet, dead drift, no drag. Patience. Wait until it sinks and then wait some more. *Bam*. It is not easy to see the fly among the foam and bubbles, but after keying your eyes on them for a few days, it is amazing how you adjust and can see it even 50 feet away. I watched as it drifted back toward me in the reverse flow of the eddy, remembering to take in line without disturbing the fly so I'd be able to strike when he bit—and he did. I had three more good ones on and then the thunder came. We packed it in.

In your pursuit of becoming a competent fly fisher, give it some time—and give yourself some time. Find the patience to stop all the flailing away and just enjoy each cast to its fullest.

—Tom McCoy

It's Really Pretty Simple . . .

Learn the meaning of "good line management," then practice it. Set the hook! Any indication of a take should trigger a hook set.

—John McMillan

Beware the Pitfalls . . . Wading Staffs Can Spook Fish

Because of the physical differences between water and air, sound waves move almost five times faster and four times farther in water than in air. If we want to be stealthy (like a Great Blue Heron), we have to be quiet. Oftentimes, we spook fish when our metal-tipped wading staffs clang off the stream's rocky bottom. A simple solution is to fit the staff with a properly sized rubber foot made for walking canes or furniture legs (a little duct tape can help to secure it). To keep the wading staff's carbide tip from poking through the rubber, drop an appropriately sized metal nut into the rubber foot to keep the carbide tip away from the bottom of the rubber. Besides being a lot quieter, the wading staff will also provide better stability on the stream bottom.

—John Mosovsky

And So Can Shadows

We all know that shadows on the water created by our moving bodies and fishing rods will spook fish. It is surprising how long these shadows can be! Under the right conditions, time, and location, we anglers can easily cast a shadow long enough to extend across the entire width of a fairly wide river. For example, a 6-foot angler, wielding a 9-foot fly rod, fishing one hour after sunrise on June 1 on the Lehigh River in Allentown, Pennsylvania, would cast a shadow 87 feet long! Not being aware of the potential to create very long shadows can definitely spoil what otherwise could be a productive fishing trip!

—John Mosovsky

Don't Overlead Rising Trout

Where would you drop your dry fly to coax a fat trout to eat it?

In water that's clear, you can't bonk the fish on the head. If you drop the fly on its nose, as if the fly literally appeared out of thin air, a trout this big will call your bluff. Besides, you don't want the splashdown, no matter how subtle, to happen where the fish can see it or, perhaps more important, hear it or feel it.

But you can take things too far in the other direction, as well, and cast a dry fly *too far* upstream. And that's the mistake I see anglers make more often than not.

Sure, I've talked about casting longer leaders as the trick for catching smart trout, and I absolutely stand by that. But casting a longer leader is a serious challenge: you need that thing to straighten out, or else you're going to create micro-drag that ruins your chances at fish. So if you can straighten out a 15-foot leader, by all means, go for it. But if you're like most anglers, and you're working with 9 to 11 feet of leader, you should focus on the "6-foot zone."

By that, I mean that the perfect cast lands 6 feet upstream of a rising trout. You don't want much more, or you risk lining the fish with your floating fly line. But much less, and you run into the splash problems I described.

Six feet is the right distance in most cases. And always, always cast to the current side of the fish, not the slack-water side.

Get in that zone, don't overlead your targets, and you will hook many, many more trout on dry flies.

—K. D.

Fish Dry Flies "Drowned"

Grasshoppers are like double cheeseburgers for trout—fatty, juicy, and packed with tasty protein. A languid hopper strike by a rising monster brown is always a thrill, but sometimes the fish just won't gorge themselves on a surface smorgasbord. When naturals are jumping off the banks but trout won't look at your fly, it doesn't necessarily mean the fish aren't eating hoppers. The smart trout—often the biggest—will wait for hoppers to sink below the surface before taking a bite.

To fish the hopper season most effectively, you must learn to fish those patterns dry—and wet. And by wet, I mean drowned.

Apply sinking grease to the hopper, and dead drift it down a seam where you think trout are holding low. You won't need a strike indicator; when a fish grabs it, you'll feel it. Or let that waterlogged pattern swing out at the end of a run, a foot or so below the surface.

The best secret for fishing drowned hoppers, however, is to weight your leader with enough split shot so you feel steady tension as your rig drifts through deeper, more turbid runs. Pinch on the amount of weight needed to have it drop like a rock, then add an extra BB. Tie a gaudy hopper on 18 inches of tippet below the weight. As you make the drift, when you feel the tension hiccup or lift, assume that a trout has inhaled the fly, and set the hook. It's an acquired feel, but this technique usually turns the biggest trout—especially during bright days in the middle of hopper season.

—K. D.

Try the *Other* Side of the Log

It's a common situation: trees fall in rivers and get pressed against or near banks. Those logs slowly rot away, and as they do, they create great holding cover for trout.

The angler—whether walking the river or floating downstream—instinctively casts flies near these logs. But what is position A? Where should the first cast go?

Well, in my experience, bigger fish tend to hold on the *shore* side of the log. So casting over the log with a dry fly is the way to go. I had always assumed that big fish held on the current side of the log, but the more I've been shooting photos and videos underwater, and the more I've been targeting

The submerged log is a trout magnet. Cast on the shore side as well as the current side—the big ones often like the slack water.

deadfall, the more I'm finding trout tucked between the log and the shoreline.

An even better way to elicit a strike in these situations is by using a streamer—but that's a tricky move: casting over a log and ripping the retrieve quickly, before the fly has a chance to sink and snag on the log.

Either way, you're going to lose some flies casting around deadfall. But if you don't hang up now and then, you aren't trying hard enough. And if you aren't throwing over the log, in many rivers you're probably missing most of the large trout.

—K. D.

Use Spinning Gear to Better Learn How to Present Flies

The best trout anglers are also bass anglers, carp anglers, pike anglers, and so on. Your mental "spice cabinet" can never be too big when you're cooking up ways to catch trout, and some of those spices cannot be obtained only on trout rivers. Some of the best fly anglers learn a lot by using swimming baits or other crossover techniques. I don't know, for example, how you can truly master Czech nymphing if you've never thrown a Carolina rig at bass.

—K. D.

Maintain a Low Profile

I know you've heard me say it before, but I will say it again: the number-one trick to catching wary trout in calm waters has nothing to do with how far you can cast, or even how well you might choose a fly pattern; it has everything to do with concealing yourself, and making a natural presentation.

Try fishing, for example, on a mountain or pasture creek where there aren't any trees to be found. The water is gin-clear. And, sure, the trout are blissfully naive to the threats any angler might pose. But you still must crawl on your belly to take a look, and, I promise you, when it is time to cast, you should never grow taller than 3 feet—it might just all happen from a kneeling (sometimes prone) position.

You may have great presentation skills. You might be able to punch a 60-footer and drop it on a dime, in a spot no larger than a place mat on the dinner table. And you might even have the most whiz-bang fly pattern ever created. But none of that matters if you barge around the riverbank

If you can make the cast from a crouch, and if you can avoid getting your boots wet . . . do it.

like a plow horse and try to enforce your will on a smart, big trout.

It all starts with stealth. No matter where you fish; no matter when you fish. And you can either take my word for it or spend the next 20 years learning the hard way.

—K. D.

Stay Out of the River!

You don't get extra points for getting your boots wet. I know, it feels nice. You get that connection to the river. But the wetter your legs are, the less your odds are of catching fish. I try to keep my boots dry, at least as much as possible. One of the best «presentation» tips is to avoid stirring up

the water and making noise/vibrations in the river. So stay out of the water.

—K. D.

A Longer Leader Catches More Trout (If You Can Cast It)

I want to be clear about something . . . 3 extra feet of leader/tippet is worth more than 30 extra feet of casting distance, in most trout-fishing situations.

Let me explain that a little more, because it is the best tip I've picked up while in New Zealand. In clear water, where you are sight fishing at defined targets, being able to cast and turn over a 15-foot leader with a 30- to 40-foot cast is far more valuable than being able to throw a fly line 60 or 70 feet to begin with, if you're going to have a 9-foot leader tied to the end of your line. And a longer 4X leader is far, far more effective than a shorter, lighter one. The longer your leader, the heavier material you can use.

Like most American anglers, I have always attached the standard 9-foot (sometimes 7.5-foot) leader straight from the package to my fly line, added a foot or two of tippet material, and set off on my merry way. And that's always worked. But it's amazing what adding just a few more feet of tippet, so that you're ultimately casting 15 feet or more of clear material, can do for your hookup ratio. It eliminates fish being spooked by the solid fly line (of any color) directly overhead. It gives you a longer drift through the zone, and it eliminates much of the drag as you present the fly—all really important keys to getting a spooky, selective trout to nab a dry fly off the surface.

The downside is that a long leader can be tricky to cast. It's hard to get it to straighten out, especially when there's even a puff of a headwind to contend with. Fight through that. Learn to throw longer leaders. Here are three tips on how to make that happen:

1. Build the right leader. It's okay to have a heavy butt section; in fact, you need that to turn the leader over. Some people use a short (6-inch) strand of Amnesia line to connect the fly line to the leader. I usually just start out with a 2X or 3X leader, and taper down from there. Try not to jump numbers, meaning, tie 2X to 3X to 4X, not 2X straight to 4X. Make sure your knots are well away from the fly, and tie good ones. (I use Blood Knots or Double Surgeon knots.) Test them before you cast.

2. In a headwind, to turn the leader over, you need to adjust your stroke to go a tad smoother on the backcast (still with authority) and harder on the forward punch. Drive the flies toward the surface, but don't crash them down. You want everything to extend about a foot above the target zone and fall down to the water from there. Drop your casting plane so the flies don't flutter in the wind.

3. Shock the tippet at the end if you have to, by making an extra-abrupt stop of the rod when you finish the cast. Sometimes you might even give the fly line a gentle two-inch tug—a "minihaul," if you will—just to turn that leader over. You'll feel it as you get the timing down. And the best way to do it right is a straight up-and-down cast. Toss the sidearm stuff out the window.

You might not always need the 15-foot leader, but trust me, learning how to cast and turn one over will never hurt you. Spend more time practicing that little move in the backyard than you spend trying to hoof out an extra 10 yards of line, and I promise you, you will hook more trout, wherever you fish, especially in clear water.

—K. D.

(Thanks to *Field & Stream* for allowing us to reprint some tips that originally ran on the "Fly Talk" blog.)

CHAPTER 5

General Tips and Tricks on Landing Fish, Handling Fish, and More

Handling Fish: The 10-Second Rule

Anglers spend a lot of time talking about catch-and-release ethics and taking grip-'n'-grin photos, keeping 'em wet, and all that stuff. I think we've done a pretty good job of getting away from grip-'n'-grins, but to be honest with you, the notion that fish won't ever get lifted out of the water for a photo is not going to happen.

So for those of you who want a good, realistic guideline, now you have it: A scientific study published in *Fisheries* boils it all down to this: If you have to lift a fish out of water, keep it limited to 10 seconds or less. Of course, a number of variables affect a fish's survival rate after being caught, such as water temperature, duration of the fight, and so on. This is a simple, straightforward guideline that everyone should be able to live by. Ten seconds. Ten Mississippi. That's it. Whether you get the shot or you don't. Not 10 seconds, fumble around with your camera, rinse the fish in the water for a few seconds, and then 10 more seconds. Ten and done. Works for me, how about you?

—K. D.

Leave Your Ego at Home

Leave your ego at home. Seek out and fish with the best fishermen that you can find and don't be intimidated. Learn from them. Put the bluster away and listen. Ask questions. Trot out that awkward cast, expose those rough technical issues, and let the more experienced anglers help. They will, I promise you.

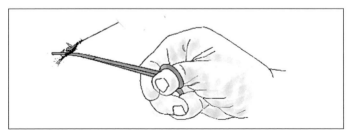

Use hemostats to pull firm your knots.

Understand that spending a lot of money and traveling great distances to fish is no guarantee of success. Quite the contrary, you're putting yourself on unfamiliar turf and placing yourself in the hands of the fates, and that often ends badly. If you can't be satisfied with the ride, if the tug is all that will make a trip successful, you might as well stay home.

—Mike Sepelak, North Carolina

Do New Anglers a Favor

As somebody who has covered fishing for more than 25 years, I have realized, hopefully not too late, that I relied too heavily on the people I was writing about. Too often, I let them tie the knots, pick the flies, and tell me where to cast. I didn't learn the way other anglers do, and it costs me when I go on my own.

Do new anglers a favor and help them just enough to get them going, but let them discover how to become a better angler for themselves. People often tell me, "you must be a great angler," and I respond, "Nope, I just know who to go with." It's the truth and sometimes the truth hurts.

—Brett Prettyman, Salt Lake City, Utah

Go Tip to Butt

Don't assemble your 4-piece rod starting at the butt and moving outward. At the end, you're either sticking the handle into the ground or supporting the entire stick at the weakest ferrule. Go the other way, tip to butt, or put the top two sections together, then the bottom, and complete construction in the middle.

—Mike Sepelak

Get in Shape

Get in shape. Because done right, fly fishing requires a healthy dose of athleticism. Not the team-player, ball-catching sort, which works out well for me, but balance, stamina, and coordination. Fishing small backcountry streams, for example, can quickly turn into a gymnastics–rock climbing combo course, and it's all-around more enjoyable if your body is used to such demands. Not to mention being in good physical shape can actually up your game on the water, enabling you to reach pockets and pools other anglers pass up for easier (safer) access. So run, hike, bike, give your dog a bonus walk (the hilly route this time). Especially when fishing the backcountry, you're a liability (or annoyance at the very least) to your fishing partner if the last time your heart got seriously pumping was walking the bleacher stairs to get to your assigned backseat-quarterbacking chair. I know I've had a good day of fishing when there are bushwhacking cuts on my face, bruises on my shins, and when I wake up with a few sore muscles the next morning.

—Erin Block, Boulder, Colorado

The Stream Not Taken

Fish places others don't. There is a difference between improving as a flyfisherman and improving your fishing. Spending time on technical, heavily pressured tailwaters can sharpen your skills finer than any other whetstone. However, the best way to improve your fishing is to fish places others don't. Hike farther and higher than the will of other anglers. Bypass the easy-to-access pools and tempting stretches of stream within sight of the road—keep going farther. Fish the gnarly places and shallow riffles others avoid or walk past without thought, because these are often places where the best fish live.

—Jay Zimmerman, Boulder, Colorado

Go Fishing

Finally, last bits and tips that I remember that made a difference: if you want to catch fish, go fishing. Thinking about it and talking about it and even reading and writing about it do NOT catch fish. The more time in the water = more fish.

—Susie Leeson, Steamboat Springs, Colorado

Breaking Down Stuck Rods

Have you ever gotten off the river, ready to pack up your gear, and, to no avail, cannot separate a rod section when breaking down your rod? It has happened recently to me. I was fishing by myself and looking around found no one else to tug on the other end of the rod. I packed up my rod, took it back to the campsite finding another person to help, but to no avail, tugging both ends did not separate! I was reminded by a fellow TU friend that packing the rod in cold (especially in the summer) may help. So I packed both sides of the rod section in ice bags for a while, and sure and behold it worked! It reminded me of my mother, who told me to pack my finger in ice while trying to remove a tight ring. That worked, too! Maybe we have more in common with our fly rods then we thought!

—Kerri Russell, Arkansas

The Healing Powers of the River

I am at the edge of the river with my fly rod in hand and ready to step into the current. The fog is lifting off the surface, and I smell the wonderful scent of the river and the moist air around me. I step into the current and am anxious to throw that first cast. Having tied on a fly that might work, I cast up river into the current, mend, and wait for a tug on the line. I am in the moment. I am not thinking about what I need to get done at work, or the house, or anything else in my life. My thoughts are on the fish. Which fly to use? Which cast to make? What part of the river to cast? I am in the moment. The current that tugs at my legs is carrying away all of the cares of my real life away and allowing me to be in the moment. This is truly the healing power of the river. At the end of the day, I am refreshed and ready to embark on what I need to get done at work, or the house, or anything else in my life. Oh, to be back on the river again.

—Kerri Russell

Hook the Damn Clip

I've spent a lot of time in waders, and I've come to the realization that, if you can get away without them, you're generally going to be better off. But I get it—trout water is cold, and in northern climes, sometimes, so is the ambient air temperature. Waders are a necessary evil.

And they can be evil. Modern waders usually come with neoprene stocking feet, and a gravel guard that slips down over your wading boot. Most of these gravel guards have little clips meant to hook onto one of the bootlaces on your wading boots. I used to be pretty lazy with waders, seeing as how I was generally ticked off that I had to wear them in the first place. (Yes, I'll be the guy wet wading the Henry's Fork on a 65-degree day in October.) So, I would just slide the gravel guard haphazardly over the tongue of my wading boots and go fishing.

Inevitably, that little clip would be the bane of my day. It is a fly-line magnet. If you cast and pile line at your feet, it's uncanny how many times the fly line will find its way into that little clip and hinder what would have been your best cast of the day. And it doesn't just fall out on its own. No. You have to stop fishing, bend over, work your fingers under the gravel guard, and force the fly line out of it. Repeatedly. The moral of the story? Hook the clip to one of your bootlaces! If it's full of a bootlace, it won't be full of fly line when you're casting to that rising rainbow 50 feet away.

—Chris Hunt, Idaho Falls, Idaho

Keep Your Rod Strung

Most of my tips were picked up from other people, so I shouldn't really claim them, but this one I had to learn for myself. Bush-whacking out of Woody Creek Canyon in the dark several years back, I stumbled and slid down a snow bank, and when I recovered, the tip of my rod was gone. Still not learning my lesson, I lost a friend's rod tip coming out of the Gunpowder in the dark. Miraculously, I was able to hike back down with a flashlight and find it in a bush. Ever since, if I'm walking through the woods before/after fishing, I make sure to keep the rod strung up.

—Keith Curley

Take Time to Soak Up the Scenery

You hear people say fishing is just an excuse to visit amazing places all the time. Too often, once we get to those special locations across the planet, we focus entirely on the fishing. Take time to soak up the scenery, to appreciate the places where native fish live, and to let wild places replenish your soul.

—Brett Prettyman

Fish "Open" Water

Don't get hung up on special-regulations water. We fly anglers tend to gravitate to sections where rules are geared to our chosen craft. Water outside "fly water" can be outstanding. We think that bait-and-gear guys hammer the water and keep a lot of the fish. Sometimes trout density can be a little thinner in "open" water. But if the water is good, there will be fish. And those fish will be used to seeing (and ignoring) bait, plugs, spoons, and spinners. But they might not be used to ignoring flies.

—Mark Taylor

Tying Leader

When tying up your leader, knot all your sections together and then trim the tag ends when you have completed the leader and tied on a fly. Of course, better to pretie most of your leaders in the off-season.

—Brian Kozminski, Boyne City, Michigan

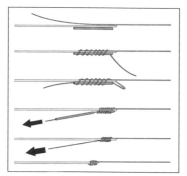

Flyline to Leader-Nail Knot

Backing to Reel-Arbor Knot

Leader to Tippet-Double Surgeon's Loop

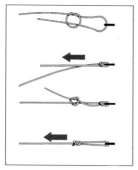

Tippet to Fly-Homer Rhode Loop Knot

Tippet to Fly-Improved Clinch Knot

Listen to Locals

Listen to your guide/locals who know. If a guide says tie on a 16 Iso nymph, I recommend you do so. Locals also have many patterns that work in their region, not going to mention names, but many have become very famous, and what works out West, may not have the same result in the Midwest.

—Brian Kozminski

Advice for the Beginning Flyfisherman: Knots 101

There has never been a better time to be a beginner flyfisherman. Fly lines and leaders come with ready-made loops, so you don't have to get bogged down with learning all the knots to get started. There really is only one knot you need to know in order to get started—and that is the one you know how to tie. For me, the uni-knot is that knot. I have fished alone many times for over 15 years knowing only one knot. It's caught trout in Colorado, bass in Texas, and redfish on the Texas Coast.

—Andy Barclay

Blood Knots and Split Shot

When I moved to Ohio from Maine, I started fishing for steelhead, which was very difficult at first. Here are some things that I learned. I used to hate the chuck and duck and how the split shot would invariably get chucked right up to the fly and this would cause the fly to drift improperly and then get snagged. The blood knot turned out to be the missing link in my quest for steelhead. I put the split shot above the last blood knot before the fly. Blood knots kept the split shot in place rather than having them constantly slide down the rig during the indelicate chucking part of the operation. By keeping the split shot in place, the flies then got a drag-free drift. Also, the blood knot can be placed at a variety of lengths above the fly in order to target fish that are on the bottom or suspended. I suppose any line could be used for building leaders, but I love the burly Germanic Maxima. It can withstand the enormous strain of a steelhead run. The way the line cinches for blood knots—well, it just feels right. I also like the creativity of fashioning my own leader—it also lets me control the length and thus the depth in a way that a tapered leader can't.

—Willard P. Greenwood II

Tips Learned over Time

I am a 30-year-plus flyfisherman. I started by buying a fly rod and books and trying to teach myself. I made many mistakes, but with the help and advice of friends and acquaintances, I eventually began catching fish. Listed below are a few tips I found to be useful:

1. Always fly fish where there are fish.
2. If you do not know the water, start fishing with a nymph.

3. Never take your wife night fishing. That is a guaranteed disaster.

—Joe Stasik

Words of Wisdom?

If your line ain't on the water, ya ain't gonna catch no fish.

If you didn't catch any fish today, that's not such a bad thing—because the fish didn't really want to be caught anyway.

—Rich Tatem

Two Knots (or Three)

Learn two knots, and learn them well—one knot to tie the fly to the tippet, and the other to tie the tippet to the leader. It doesn't matter which knot you choose; the idea is to practice those two knots until you are adept at tying them.

If you are learning a knot for the first time, I suggest you use the handle on a coffee mug as the "eye" of the hook and a shoestring as the tippet. This way you can "see" what the tippet is supposed to do and can learn how to adapt the directions. Then you can work your way down to using fishing line and eventually tippets.

I suggest that the surgeon's knot be used for tippet to leader connections—fairly easy to tie and has good knot strength. If you haven't been tying lures to fishing line (and hence know a knot you can tie), I suggest an improved clinch. Although personally, I use the Pitzen, also known as a 16-20 knot.

How the knot is tied is important; wetting the knot before tightening is critical. Nylon and Fluorocarbon are thermoplastics. The friction of rubbing together during the setting of the knot will affect the thickness of the tippet, and thus decrease the strength of the knot.

If there are break offs while fishing (either snag or fish), check where the break occurs. If it is at or near the knot—think about what might be going on to degrade the line at that point. It could be just small nicks on the tippet from fish teeth or rocks. Also, it's a good idea to check the tippet for rough spots every once in a while. If roughness is felt, tie on new tippet or leader. If wind knots are found, replace  the tippet or leader. It could also be bad knot-tying technique.

Some folks want to tie a good, nonslip loop in their tippet or leader. If so, I recommend the surgeon's loop. A straightforward expansion on the surgeon's knot. So most of the same skillset is involved. It is a "third" knot to learn and hopefully builds enough confidence so people can explore other knots.

—Milt Lane, St. Louis, Missouri

Use a Guide

If traveling a long distance or going to a new fishing location, use a guide. They know the waters and best flies. Your chances of success are much better and it is well worth the extra money.

Keep notes on your fishing trips—the pluses and minuses. Review them the next time you go and be sure to practice your casting. The reviews and practice can help you get back into the "groove" much quicker and increase your chances of success.

—Dan Beistel, Oviedo, Florida

The Best Advice I Ever Got

The Problem:

When stringing a line on your rod, who hasn't reached the tip only to drop the line and then watch it fall all the way down through all the eyes?

The Solution:

Double over the end of the line as you push it through the eyes. If you drop it, it will catch and not fall through the eyes.

Saves a lot of frustration and some language!

—Forrest Wood, Redmond, Washington

Play the Banjo to Clear Weeds

Ever get gunk and weeds on your tippet or leader? Of course. We all do. But rather than using your fingers to try to pick the mess off your fly, or weight, or the knots connecting the leader to the tippet (places where weeds and gunk collect) simply stretch out the tippet, and use your thumb to pluck it, as if you're plucking the string of a banjo. The vibration will cause the weeds to fly right off. It's faster, cleaner, and easier to clean your tippet this way than any other.

—Jon Christiansen, Mequon, Wisconsin

173

Get Informed

When visiting a distant area, go to the nearest fly shop and hire a guide for the day. He knows what the fish are doing and can put you way ahead of the game. If you can't afford it, then ask where, when, and how to fish the places they put you onto. Then buy some flies and thank him for the information.

—Carl Wachter

Plan and Call Ahead

My tips were learned the hard way . . . a 2-hour ride to find a washed-out stream, a broken rod at the peak of an evening sulphur hatch, and arriving streamside before dawn and spending the next 20 minutes stringing up the fly rod and tying on the leader and tippet!

Call a tackle shop located in the area you are traveling to for stream conditions. Nothing is worse than driving two hours to find a washed-out stream.

Pack an extra rod, reel, and waders. You never know when a break or major tear will occur.

String up your rod and reel. Tie on leaders and tippets while still at home. It will save precious fishing time!

—Jim Gazze

Finding Leaks

When waders leak, turn them inside out and rub an alcohol-wet rag over the area of the small leak and the hole will show up as a purple spot. You can then repair using standard repair glue right over the leaking area.

—Tom Morehouse, Orinda, California

Albolene Cream

Want a very good, very economical floatant? Buy Albolene cream found in a drugstore. Originally a face moisturizer, it works exactly like a floatant, at 10 percent of the price.

—Tom Morehouse

Quick Dry a Waterlogged Dry Fly

The next time you find a packet of SILICA GEL desiccant in a mail-order package, save it. Cut it open and pour some into your mini–coffee bean grinder. Grind it to a powder. Put the powder into an old plastic film tube (everyone saved these handy little containers). When your fly will no longer float, drop it, tippet attached, into the container. After a shake or two, pop it out, flick it with your fingernail, and you will have a fly as dry as the day you tied it.

—Kent Heiliger

Nature's Own Ferrule Grease

Although I have never seen it in a fly shop, I hear from other people that ferrule grease is something you can actually purchase. A great way to keep ferrules from sticking and to protect your ferrules from additional wear that comes from putting your rod together and taking it down is to take your thumb and forefinger and touch the bridge of your nose—grab a little bit of "Nature's Ferrule Grease"—and rub it on your ferrules. No cost, nothing extra to pack. Never have trouble disconnecting fly rod sections again.

—Jim Long, Littleton,
Colorado

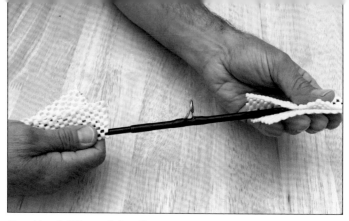

Use rubber shelf liners to help pull stuck rods apart.

New Use for Shelf Liner

To take apart your fly fishing rod, simply cut two pieces of non-slip shelf liner and use them to grip the rod sections, then twist and pull carefully.

—Luis Rincones, Miami, Florida

Tie Them on at Home

As I have grown older, flies have not grown bigger and trout sometime still want small flies. My solution for fishing sizes 20 to 26? At my tying bench where I can use my jewelry magnifiers,

I tie a snelled tip on the fly and a loop in my leader, so I can use them easily when in midstream. Changing patterns is now a snap and not 30 minutes of frustration.

—Hector I. Macedo

Rod Condoms

You know how you and your buddies' fly rods get all tangled when you put them in the hatchback to travel between wading sites on the Yellowstone? I cut sections out of one of those retracting slinky-hoses, and the Cordura makes great sleeves. I make them no more than four feet long, taper-cut the ends to facilitate slipping on and off. On some I put Velcro on the end to allow them to grab and slip off from inside the car compartment. I showed these to Craig Mathews, and he was thinking of making them to solve

a problem we all encounter when driving from place to place on the rivers.

—Zygmunt J. B. Plater,
Newton Centre,
Massachusetts

Fly Vest–Pocket Divider

I can double the usefulness of some pockets by inserting a plastic divider I cut out of a plastic milk container. Punching a hole in the bottom and sewing it down at the base keeps it

Try a homemade vest pocket divider.

from slipping up and out.

Hook and Barbless fly nest.

I can have both a fly box and a forceps or tippet reel in the same pocket without tangling.

—Zygmunt J. B. Plater

Barbless Hook Fly Nest

For the past 30 years, I've solved the problem of having my used flies with barbless hooks slipping off a sheepskin patch by sewing a nylon net bag with an elastic hem in front of the sheepskin, with Velcro backing to stick onto a Velcro patch sewn on my vest. In the evening, I take the nest off the vest and pull out and clean the flies.

—Zygmunt J. B. Plater

License Pockets on Fly Boxes

As the years go by and my plethora of fly-fishing gear continues to grow, I constantly find myself trying to simplify my system so that it is as efficient and effective as possible. Trying to be a well-rounded angler takes a lot of different, specialized equipment, and from day to day I am switching out rods, reels, boxes, vests, sling packs, lanyards, and even boats. No matter what sort of trip I am on, two things cannot be left behind: a fly box and a fishing license. At the beginning of the season, I print out a number of extra copies of my license and create little individualized pockets on all of my fly boxes to store them. In order to do this, I use scissors, packaging tape, and a Ziploc bag. I simply cut the plastic bag into a rectangular shape and tape it on three sides to the outside of my fly box, creating a nice little pocket for the licenses. (Those little plastic holders that many sports stores provide licenses in work even better.) I have wasted far too much fishing time rummaging around through my vest, sling pack, or backpack trying to find my license. Now all I have to do is grab the fly box of the day, and the license comes with it. It is a simple, logical tip that makes things a whole lot more convenient.

—Adam Lucas

Homemade Lanyard

Being that I am not one for extravagance, instead of splurging on one of the many gaudy (my opinion), bead-filled, braided, elaborate lanyards currently on the market, I decided to hit my local sporting-goods store and grab a coach's lanyard for $3.99. Throw aside the whistle or save it for coaching, tie a couple of loop knots, and you are ready to go. I attach my tippet caddy to the clasp, clamp on forceps, tie on an old cork (to hold a few flies) and some floatant, and I am all set. Feel free to add some electronic packing foam for a neck pad, and a small clip toward the bottom to fasten it to your shirt. Old fly-line backing is what I use to tie on my accessories. It isn't overly pretty, but it works well, and its simplicity is refreshing in the ever-increasing complexity of the fly-fishing world.

—Adam Lucas

How to Land Big Trout in Two Minutes or Less

The faster you can land a trout, the better.

How you handle fish after you catch them is critical to their survival. If you're going to be a catch-and-release angler, you must do it right. But science tells us that how you fight a fish—specifically, how long it takes—is also a key factor in whether it survives after having been caught. The longer the fight, the more lactic acid builds up, which can be lethal for a fish. This is why I always cringe when people talk about catching large trout,

When a trout's head comes up, it loses all leverage. Keep the pressure, don't lose that advantage, and you can slide it right into the net.

and the first question always seems to be "How long did it take to land it?" It's almost as if the longer the fight takes, the better.

I get that epic fights are what memories are made of, but here's a dirty little secret: it shouldn't take the average angler more than two minutes to land a trout that's up to 2 feet long. Sure, river currents and other factors matter a lot. But all things considered, from take to net, the fight should be no more than two minutes—tops.

How do you get that done?

1. **Use heavier tippet.** The more I fish, the more I realize that a trout is more likely to eat a good drift on 3X tippet than it is a cruddy drift on 7X.
2. **Don't leave your reel in free spool.** Find a good drag setting that matches your tippet size, and stick to it.
3. **Steer the fish toward the net with the rod tip pointed toward the water.** Sure, you start the fight with the rod tip high, but you steer the trout with the tip low.
4. **When the fish's head breaks the surface, don't ease up.** A trout pointed down is still a fighter, but once they go chin above the waterline, they're toast. They have no leverage, and you can steer them right into the net, so long as you keep their head up. The mistake most people make is to relinquish that advantage and let the trout tilt down. Sometimes, the head is up in a matter of seconds. The fight should be over soon after that.

You might not get as much play time, but the trout, and the other anglers, will thank you for it.

—K. D.

Toothpick Knot Tamer

Plastic serrated toothpick (ends are textured and bristled).

Goes where fingers can't.

Lightweight line saver tool.

Lasts a long time.

Carry a few. The brand I like the best: Dentek.

Fishing in the wind is always a challenge.

We all get those wind knots and tangles, sometimes tangled so tightly that cutting out the mess and retying is quicker and less irritating.

But when the tangle is of different size loops and crossovers, and the leader/tippet is worth saving, I find the smallest open knot, push the smooth point through and start the separation, getting a bigger loop that I can now put my finger(s) into, move the pick to another loop, and if necessary use the serrated end to catch the line and pull it up and through or over, repeating the untangling until my line is again ready to cast.

Takes patience but is worth doing to save a newly attached tapered leader.

—Michael C. Harrington

The Toes Know!

Thirty to 45 degrees. Fishing in the winter, early spring, feet get cold in a short amount of time, reducing the day of fishing.

I wade to my spot, get my feet placed and spaced for forward casting, then turn my boots, resetting left or right to the current that is now breaking against the side of my boots, NOT my toes that would be normally taking the cold water directly. Once the toes get cold, it's pretty much an uncomfortable feeling.

My cast can still be over the shoulder but balance is dicey, so I do a chest cross cast or a side arm waist cross cast just like I would cast over the shoulder, still laying out the line to the fish.

I also wear a heavier all-wool, thigh-high sock and a silk liner sock in a one-size-larger boot for my winter fishing, and I can stay in the water a half day until lunch time.

—Michael C. Harrington

Use a Bobber to Make Knots and Rigs

I have a tip that I have never seen anywhere else. I fish a lot of double-nymph rigs and dry droppers. Attaching the dropper fly, you must attach the tippet to the lead fly. This can be a pain for some people, I found a way to make an easy loop to attach the tippet to the hook shank of the lead fly. This has cut my time tying knots and allowed more time for my fly in the water, where it belongs. It's very simple: take a bobber like we bream fish with. The weighted cigar foam bobber, about two or three inches long, two-to-three inch size works best and fits the hand well. The bobber must be the clip-on type. These bobbers can be fixed on the line, via the clip. Much like a pair of hackle pliers, however, the clip can be turned and line can freely move through the bobber clip. This is the side we use to make the loop. Run your tippet through the bobber clip, again the open part of the clip, not in a fixed position. (I do not clip my tippet from the spool while making this knot. I got tired of dropping them in the stream after clipping from the spool. It can be cut to size after you finish the knot and then attach the fly.) Pass about 6 to 18 inches tippet through clip. The bobber will hang now. Holding both sides of tippet, simply tie a uni-knot. Wet knot and as you pull down, hold your thumb and finger above the bobber on the tippet. Pull the knot down to the fingers, but not all the way to the bobber clip. Pull the tag end also. The knot will tighten, but not all the way. Now push the button on the bobber that raises the clip and release the knot. Now you have a small loop that can be easily placed over the hook of the lead fly. Tighten the knot and trim. This is very quick and easy, although my explanation of it may not sound that way. You can also use the bobber much like a Ty-Rite tool for tying a clinch knot. For this, you use the fixed side of the bobber clip to hold the hook while turning the bobber about 5 turns and then run the tippet back through the loop to finish the clinch knot.

—Andy Pendl

Dress Flies So You Can See Them

I have been a fly-fishing guide since 2001 and a member since 1996 and vice president of the Northern Virginia Chapter for many years. I have been giving a presentation to our local fly-fishing community, as well as speaking at several TU chapters in Virginia and Maryland on the topic of "More time fishing, less time with equipment." It is a collection of tips that I have learned not only from my own fly-fishing experience, but from other anglers and guides over the years. It consists of about 25 tips, but the one that has been most helpful to me—because I am firmly entrenched in what I like to call the march of time and so are my clients for the very same reason (eyesight isn't what it used to be)—is . . . if you are dry-fly fishing and using small flies (Tricos, BWOs, Midges, and small ants), I like to apply a floatant, then brush on Frogs Fanny or another desiccant; and, instead of blowing it off, leave it on it, which makes for a big fluffy target that you can see for days. It has been so helpful with my clients, who now can see the drift of the fly.

—Kathleen "Kiki" Galvin

How Much Gear Should I Carry?

In the old days, a new flyfisherman might have had a handful of flies that he kept in a metal Sucrets box. He carried a pocket-knife and went fishing. No fancy vest or even a formal fly box. No tippet spools, nippers, knot tools, or leader straighteners.

When I got into the sport, I bought some metal fly boxes that looked like the expensive ones the real fishermen had, soon followed by a vest. In not too long a time, the vest began to fill with all kinds of gadgets, leaders, tippet spools, flashlights, insect repellent, strike indicators, split shot—so much stuff.

The number of fly boxes grew and grew as the fly collection expanded. Soon the pockets, as ample as they were, bulged so much, I could rest my rod across my vest on the shelves they created. I looked like the Michelin man.

I would rearrange the content of the pockets each season, eventually settling on this one for nymphs, that one for streamers, mayflies over here, and caddis over there. I literally carried every fly I owned every time I fished.

Eventually, I just had too much stuff and also became more aware of seasonal fly choices. I began to keep a gym bag of fly boxes and all that extra stuff. I put what I thought I would need on a particular outing into the vest, leaving the rest in the bag.

Without fail, I would get on the stream and feel the need for something I left in the car. I was still struggling with that common perception that it is the tackle that will catch the fish rather than the fisherman.

Much later in my career, I began to minimize. I tried a few different versions of chest and sling packs. Some were more complicated than the vest; they were quickly discarded. I like the newer sling packs and have one set up for steelhead and salmon fishing.

My current trout pack is small. Very small. In fact, I could easily carry what is in it in my shirt pockets, eliminating the pack altogether. The reason I don't is I like to grab the pack and go, knowing I have the essentials—a nipper, spare leader, three tippet spools, floatant, forceps, a thin box of nymphs, a small streamer wallet, and one dry-fly box that also holds terrestrials.

The streamers and nymphs are the same most of the time: Woolly Buggers in green and black, Mickey Finn, Grey Ghost, Black Nosed Dace, and some buggy-looking things from Montana for streamers; Pheasant Tail, Prince, Copper John, and Gold Ribbed Hare's Ears, a couple of stoneflies, plus a few more nymphs.

I fill the dry-fly box with whatever I think I will need for that day. It holds the standards on one side—a few Adams in a variety of sizes, some BWOs, a couple of caddis, ants, and favored attractors. The other side depends on the season, the water, the location. In springtime, it is filled with Hendricksons, Grey Fox Variants, March Browns, and Iso's, for example. Sulphurs, Cahills, and hoppers are added in June.

The pack is about 8 × 6 × 3 inches and is on a long strap so I can put it behind me when fishing.

I am freed of the weight, bulk, and discomfort of a vest. More important, I am now challenged with figuring out how

to catch fish with what I have. Location, presentation, and patience.

I continue to work on my minimizing and am enjoying the simplification. Not down to a Sucrets box yet but maybe . . .

—Tom McCoy

Don't Hog a Hole

Don't be a bear, don't hog a hole. If you've caught a few fish in a good spot and others are fishing nearby, move on and give them a shot.

—John McMillan

Safety Item

I fish in the southern Appalachian Mountains a lot. A guide on the Hiwassee once told me the most important piece of equipment you can take onto a stream is a whistle. The frequency of a whistle carries over the roar and sounds of a mountain stream. A handy thing to have in the case of an emergency and you are trying to get someone's attention. I carry a whistle on my lanyard.

—Mike Bryant, Tennessee

Another Safety Item

After slipping and falling on a large rock on a high-mountain stream that broke my bursa sac behind my kneecap, I now wear thin knee pads to protect my knees. The pads also come in handy when kneeling to keep a low profile.

—Mike Bryant

Plan to Learn

I purposely and consciously try to learn something new every time I go fishing. Whether working on my drift, testing a new fly, or reading the water, I always think about what I will focus on before going out to the stream. It's a great way to continuously build your skills (and enjoyment) over a long life of fly fishing.

—Mike Bryant

Clinch Knot Made Easy

For 55 years, I have struggled with the clinch knot. After twisting the tag end around the main line, I would struggle with getting the tag back through that tiny hole between the lines that came off the eye of the hook. It dawned on me one day to put my finger on the eye of the hook and make the twists above my finger. When I was done with the twists, I took my finger out and had a large hole that was very easy to put my tag end through. I made my tag end plenty long so it would be easy to grasp. So as not to waste leader, after getting the tag end through the hole, I then snug the line with a little pulling on the knot to get the tag end short enough where I can then cut off the smallest amount possible. With eyes not as strong as they used to be, this is a great way to tie this knot, or others that use the same principle, easily and with less frustration, which I don't need when the fish are rising and I am in a hurry to get a fly tied to my tippet. I have shared this simple idea with others, and they always say, "Why didn't I think of that!"

—Bob Kowal

A Trick to Tie on Very Small Flies

I have recently been interested in fishing very small flies, size 22s and smaller. I fish the San Juan River in New Mexico, where a size 22 is a BIG fly! Even though I have 3x glasses to help me tie them on, I have simplified the process even more by tying a two-foot tippet onto the fly at my leisure. I take a 1-foot piece of material, such as a firm piece of Ethafoam or a piece of black foam water pipe insulation or similar and hook the fly on one end. Then I carefully wrap the end of the leader around it once. With a rubber band encircling my foam material, I put the other end of the tippet under it to secure it. I tie a loop in the tippet end and then use a loop-to-loop attachment to my leader. This has saved me lots of frustration when I need to tie on a fly quickly. Size 28s and 30s are a challenge no matter what size magnifiers I use.

—Bob Kowal

Fly Tube

To keep the flies from snagging on my vest, I put the foam tube into a 2-gallon Ziploc bag. If you have a long tubular plastic bag, that would work just as well. If you want to get fancy, find a lightweight aluminum tube, or even a cardboard tube you cover with water-resistant urethane, and put the foam in that and then glue an attachment point to it and put a piece of cord on it to secure it to your vest.

—Bob Kowal

How to Keep Flies and Other Fishing Gear Safe

I hate losing boxes of flies, so I do two things. One is tying a piece of 40- to 50-pound test mono to the box by going around the inside of the hinges, or some boxes have a place to attach a cord. I then secure the other end to the zipper of the pocket in my vest or one of the rings on my vest. A very small keychain clip or split ring would make it easy to take them on or off the zipper.

Second, I put my email address on a piece of adhesive tape or sticky label and stick it to my fly boxes, my rods, my reels (on the foot), and other things I don't want to lose. I cover the label with a couple layers of waterproof Scotch tape.

—Bob Kowal

Make a Rod Tube

Sometimes you want a rod case for an unusual length that is not standard. Many people use the heavier PC pipe, which works, but I like a lighter case. I make a lightweight but strong one from the plastic tubes that fluorescent light bulbs come in. Cut to length making allowance for the end caps. Use the end caps, put foam in it, and glue it into the tube at the end you will not open. For the opening, I put foam in the cap and then run a piece of cord through it and attach it to a piece of light wood, or something similar, to secure the cap when

I take it off. The other end I tie to the tube and cover it with Gorilla tape (made in America and the best duct tape). Then I use the duct tape, spiraling it around the tube in one direction to the far end of the tube, and then start from the other end and wrap back to the starting end in the opposite wrapping direction. This will give it strength and make it nearly unbendable. You can add another layer for more strength. If you want a fancier look, get someone to make a cloth sock to put around the case. One man in our Spokane fly club even designed a reel foot pocket with the cloth case, including a Velcro piece that allowed the reel cap to attach and come off easily. I carried mine on a 7-day backpacking trip into the Seven Devils Wilderness in Idaho, and my rod never got a scratch.

—Bob Kowal

Practice Palming Your Reel

In recent years, drag technologies in fly reels have gotten so good that they tend to take the necessity of "palming" (using your hand or fingers to slow the reel rim as the fish pulls line) out of the game. But as I have gravitated back to more "retro" click-and-pawl reels, I find myself revisiting that move more and more. After all, it's how many of us started playing fish, and as you get it dialed in, it actually helps you sense a fish's moves, get a better feel for when they tire and are ready to be landed, and so forth. Beyond that, palming is fun, and it helps you feel more "connected" to the fish you're battling.

In my mind, there's really no right or wrong way to palm. The one thing I'll say is that it's important to cradle the reel from the bottom, rather than the side. But you probably don't need

The art of palming a reel has been largely lost due to disc-drag technology. But try it sometimes. It will make you a better fish fighter.

me to tell you that: get your knuckles knocked by a screaming reel once or twice, and you'll smell what I'm cooking.

I also subscribe to a less-is-more approach to palming, in that I usually won't go right for the palm until after a fish has made a run on its own, and after that, I err on the side of a light touch, rather than clamping down with a grip.

Of course, you can't palm every reel, since some models have the spool fully contained within the rim. I tend to shy away from those, though, because I like to have the option of palming.

Give it a try the next time you're out (unless you plan on pulling on a hundred-pound tarpon). Even if you use a performance disc-drag reel, let it off a bit, not quite to free-spool, and start playing around with palming. After all, not everything you hook will be the exact same size or have the same energy. Also, water currents differ from spot to spot, so it's hard to dial in on an exact, do-all drag setting for every fish and every place. On top of that, in my guiding experience, a lot of anglers break off fish when they're fumbling around to adjust the drag setting. Better to set it fairly light, and to be able to use your palm to slow the reel down (at least for trout), than to have the drag too firm and hope you can back it off before you break. Palming the reel, even every now and then, will improve your fish-fighting senses immensely. That said, don't go overboard. If a performance drag will help you land a great fish, by all means, you should get what you paid for.

—K. D.

Cast with Your Nondominant Hand

It's always a benefit for an angler to be able to cast with their off hand. Whether you're sharing a drift boat and you don't want the line whizzing over the rower in the middle, or you are working around a brushy bank that forces casts to one side only, whatever. But how do you train yourself to do that? Simply use your dominant hand to cradle the reel as you cast with your off hand. The dominant hand will dictate tempo and timing (which is what the cast is really all about) and also help prevent you from drifting back too far or overcocking the wrist. Eventually, you will be able to take off the training wheels and let fly with either hand. Give it a try. You'll immediately see how it works.

—K. D.

CHAPTER 6

Paying It Forward:
Tips on Being a Trout Mentor

Twelve Tips for the Trout-Fishing Mentor

Over the years, I've picked up many tips that have helped my own angling pursuits. But I've found that the most important factor that helped me become a better flyfisherman was teaching *others* to fish. Guiding. Writing stories about it. Mentoring young people. Because it's one thing to glean a tip or a trick yourself, but when you slow down and explain it in a way that somebody else (especially a young person) can clearly understand, you reinforce those lessons with stronger cement in your own brain.

Teaching trout fishing is the ultimate win-win. You pass along a craft, a tradition, and a respect for species and wild places. In return, you get better. With that in mind, we asked a number of "angling professionals" what they thought were their most valuable tips when it came to teaching fly fishing. Their collective answers were all very interesting (considering the sources) and these tips that follow can help you on your own path of mentoring—and becoming a better angler.

1. Make It Fun

Have fun. Skip stones. Check out the cool bugs under the rocks. Catch crawfish. Swim. Then, teach them to cast. Be positive. Let them hold the fish. Laugh.

—Chris Wood, president and CEO of Trout Unlimited

Throw rocks, turn over rocks, chase frogs. Kids love discovery and having fun doing it. Let them learn how and why it all works. Simplicity is king. When my kids were young, I took a 3-weight fly rod, slipped a rod and a half-length of line out the tip, and then looped it through again so it couldn't get longer or shorter and had them pick up and lay down a nymph in a riffle of a stocked stream with eager truck trout waiting. Not too much trouble they could get into there as far as tangles

and frustrations go. They both (in their 20s now) caught their first fly-rod fish that way. Today we have tenkara rods that sort of do the same thing sans the reel. I think the loop through the tip top method makes them feel more like they have a grown-up rig in their hand, but then again, maybe it doesn't really matter to anyone else but the grown-up. The most important thing to keep in mind is that at first, you can go fishing or you can take a kid fishing, but you can't do both at the same time.

—Joe Demalderis,
Cross Current Guide Service & Outfitters

I have taught hundreds of kids / young people in my career. I have learned that the most important thing is to simply keep it fun. Being outdoors is fun, but so is practicing indoors. Casting a fly rod is the ultimate fun. Catching the fish is the "by-product" of their learning and their diligence.

—Van Rollo, owner of Mountain Sports Products

A good way to get a young child into fly fishing is to not try to get them into fly fishing. Do show them how much fun mud and creeks are (even if you have to get dirty), dig some worms, chase some crawfish, and throw a stone or two. Just be sure to have a fly rod lying around somewhere.

—Jay Zimmerman, author, guide, and noted fly tier

2. Eliminate Pressure

Try not to put a kid in a position where that first cast will be the only one that counts. Experienced fly guys are so used to situations where that first drift of a dry or swing of a streamer is going to be the producer. But for a kid, that's a lot of pressure. If they flub it, they might not brush it off. It can hurt morale too much, and I think it can also frustrate the teacher, which is never good.

—Joe Cermele, Fishing Editor, *Field & Stream*

Above all, fishing should be a safe refuge for fun. We don't talk about troubles we're having, or focus on mistakes that are being made. If my kid hits the water, with the exception of safety issues, she knows that this will be a lighthearted, fun event. Lose a fifth fly in the same tree . . . who cares? If she drops her Snickers bar in the river, I'll probably give her half of mine.

—Kevin Morlock, Indigo Guide Service, Michigan

3. Stack the Deck

The most important thing in teaching anything—sitting to dogs, music to kindergartners, fly fishing to young people—is setting them up for success. From location to gear, make it easy for kids to succeed. Get them hooked before making them work.

—Erin Block, author, and editor-at-large of *Trout*

When you take a young child out on the water, you must deliver action and success. Solitude, tranquility, and quiet casting are things that are only appreciated later in life. When you're a kid, you want results and you want to catch fish! Set your kids up in situations where they'll catch fish right away. If it takes a worm, a bobber, and a Spiderman Zebco rod, that's great. Avoid the technical spring creek and instead head to the local pond that is stuffed with bluegills and bass. Kids will love what is fun, and for kids, catching fish is fun.

—Jim Klug, director of operations,
Yellow Dog Flyfishing Adventures

Take the newbie somewhere where she/he can catch fish. I made the mistake of trying to introduce my younger daughter to fishing at a spot where the trout weren't in the mood. After an hour, her attention was gone . . . and it's been hard to get her back in the saddle.

—Chris Santella, author of *50 Places to Fly Fish Before You Die*

The key to getting the young connected is taking them to a stocked pond to ensure strikes on any fly with any presentation.

—Paul Zabel, photographer,
business consultant, Telluride, Colorado

Stocked ponds are awesome for kids. The main idea is to get out there, capture their attention, and catch some fish.

—Johnny Spillane, Olympic silver medalist, owner of Steamboat Fly Fisher

Put a rod in her hand and make sure she catches a fish. All the rest will come.

—Ed Rice, founder of the International Sportsmen's Expo and member of the California Outdoors Hall of Fame

4. Don't Limit This to Fly Fishing . . . or Trout

The first fly-fishing experience needn't be with a fly rod. Don't be afraid to stick a fly on the end of a spinning rod with a bobber. Focus on panfish, sometimes even over trout. A love of trout will come, but nothing gets a kid to fall in love with fishing faster than an afternoon of catching a couple dozen fish. And that is often the realm of bluegill and crappie . . . not trout.

—Tom Bie, editor of *The Drake* magazine

Don't get all hung up on terminal gear. When he or she is 4, a Spiderman rod and a bobber and worm is totally appropriate technology. The mission here is to catch fish and have fun. As time goes on, the tackle changes and we kill fewer fish. But I haven't had a kid yet who was interested in just picking up a fly rod and flogging the water. There's a natural progression, I think, from worm drowner / fish killer to fly angler /conservationist. But you gotta start them where they are.

—Walt Gasson, director of TU-Endorsed businesses

5. Be a Part of the Process

Just take them fishing. Spend time with them outdoors. Expose them to nature. Teach them a reverence for the natural world. The fly fishing will soon follow.

—Conway Bowman, author, television host

As a parent/adult, be involved! Most kids under the age of 16 still look up to their parents and want the adult to teach them new things. My father knew little about fly fishing, but he taught me his knowledge, and more important, he was involved (hands-on) in my learning. I really looked forward to the time together with my father, and I fell in love with fishing.

—Paul Martinez, guide, Angler's Covey,
Colorado Springs, Colorado

6. Accept That Interests Change with Age

One of the most important nuggets I gleaned when writing my book *Family Friendly Fly Fishing* was that kids' motivations and interests change about the time they reach puberty. So when they are younger, it is all about making it simple, catching fish, short days with lots of excitement, and plans for side trips for catching frogs or turtles. I can't think of a better method for younger kids than a tenkara rod on a dock for sunfish. Once they reach puberty, it seems the world changes drastically, and they are intrigued by the complexity of fly fishing. Think entomology, reading the water, etc. I think teenagers are even more interested in the complexities than adults.

—Tom Rosenbauer, author,
marketing manager, Orvis Rod & Tackle

7. Instill a Practice and *Patience* Ethic

Teaching fly fishing is the same as trying to teach someone patience. Relating that to any sport they might be interested in, the more practice, the better they will become.

—Al Keller, noted tarpon and
redfish guide, television personality

Keep the rod strung and by the back door with a practice line. Simply cast five minutes per day. Amazing results!

—Gregg Arnold,
IGFA world record holder,
Louisiana redfish guide

My daughter, Quinn, is 6 years old; I have a Joan Wulff fly rod that we practice with. I have her cast in the living room to sneakers, and we pretend they are trout!

—Al Quattrocchi, artist,
California fishing tournament director

I know it's silly, but I swear for the little people, the Orvis Practicaster works wonders. I've had Mabel on that thing in the backyard just as a game while we're hanging outside for BBQs, etc., and she loves it. It totally gives her the idea of loading a rod, and the idea of fishing is planted in her head over and over.

—Tim Romano, managing editor,
Angling Trade, and frequent *Trout* contributor

The "Photarium" keeps the fish wet as you snap photos.

Always watch your back-cast! Turn your head and see what the line is doing in relation to your rod path, stopping point, and so on. You can't come forward until the back is perfect. I related this to my dad when I was learning to drive a car. He would always say turn your head and don't rely on the mirrors. You already know what's in front of you; it's from behind or the side that can sneak up and get you.

—Tyler Palmerton, Alaska/
Washington/Oregon guide
and sales professional

8. Lead by Example

I think that each of us, as a parent or grandparent, must lead by example. We simply have to take our children to places we love and show them how to fish. If they see us having a great time and we offer an opportunity to help them fish, as well, then I think it is a natural. And, for our family anyway, it is about more than the fish. It is about making a connection with a place we care for and are inspired by. Observing the stream, learning something about its nature, and observing the beauty.

—Jack Williams, PhD, TU senior scientist

9. Make it THEIRS

I can think of two tips to get young adults interested in fly fishing. The first tip is aspirational. Young people should be told that that learning to fly fish gives them entry into a skilled community of men and women who gracefully, knowledgeably, and peacefully interact with beauty in the natural world. The second tip is practical (and when combined with tip number one, made me a flyfisherman). Young adults should be given a size 14 Royal Wulff and the opportunity to cast it into a freestone stream—preferably on public land—until they learn for themselves how to catch a trout, and the glory of it. The feeling of ownership of figuring it out for themselves is the sport's greatest bond.

—Nate Schweber, author, freelance writer,
and frequent contributor to *Trout*

Give them their own tackle from the first contact with the water, so they can feel free to use it, enjoy it, and even break it without fear, while they get the spirit of the environment. If they want just to play near the water, let them do it; it's the way for a kid to get in love with nature. If the waters conquer their hearts, they will easily learn how to fish.

—Marcelo Perez, founder and CEO of
Untamed Angling, Santa Cruz, Bolivia

10. Make a Natural Connection

Fly fishing should be positioned more about the river/stream/ lake/environment than about the catch. Oftentimes, we try to position the sport as a way to hold a fish in front of a camera. However, it is best positioned as a sport for the curious. Talk about the vast and complex ecosystem these fish live in. Find fish in strange places (about every body of water has them) and how they relate to the larger world. The notion of curiosity has so much more lasting power than the reward of holding a fish. If a young angler can become curious about the world we all love (the physical world or, even, the metaphysical), then they will be an angler forever.

—Rich Hohne, brand communications manager,
Simms Fishing Products

11. Know Your Student

Have a good idea of what the student already knows. All too often, young aspiring anglers feel disrespected by older anglers, and that kind of "listen to me, kid" sort of approach. Nothing turns off a young angler faster than disrespect based solely on age. Reverse ageism. Maybe the 16-year-old can already cast and needs help with distance, etc. The instructor needs to listen and watch a lot more than they typically do.

—Franklin Tate, director of
TU's Headwaters Youth Program

12. Ask Them Questions

It's a game you can play without even getting your boots wet. Sometimes my wife and I will stand on a bridge over-looking a river (because she has heard me talk about this waaaaaaay too much), and I'll say, "So you're the fish . . . where would you be?" and she'll point out a slick or an eddy line, and I'll say, "That's right . . . that's where I'd be, too." I think that's a game even young kids can play before they fish.

—Will Rice, writer and guide, Denver, Colorado

If I were to add my own best "teaching" tip, it would be to lead with questions. Ask the little angler, "Where do you think the fish will be?" "What do you think it will eat?" "Why do you feel that way?" "How should we cast at that fish?" At that point, you become a collaborator and a teammate, rather than another older person telling them what to do. Sure, it's good to teach fundamentals, just like with algebra, or musical scales. It's good to have credibility and instruct with authority. But the greatest impact you can impart on an angler of any age is to inspire them to use their own quizzical mind and follow their gut instincts. Besides, I've been all over the world, caught more fish than I can remember, rubbed shoulders with the most dec-orated guides and instructors on the planet . . . and sometimes, the "wisdom" of an eight-year-old girl trumps all of that. The older we get, and the more we fish, the more we realize there is still so much to learn. And sometimes, the greatest lessons come from unlikely teachers. Keep an open mind and you'll see how teaching can indeed be the key to learning.

—K. D.

Kirk Deeter is the Vice President / Editor-in-Chief of the Trout Media group of Trout Unlimited.